the WISDOM of
STABILITY

ROOTING FAITH IN A MOBILE CULTURE

JONATHAN WILSON-HARTGROVE
FOREWORD BY KATHLEEN NORRIS

PARACLETE PRESS
BREWSTER, MASSACHUSETTS

The Wisdom of Stability: Rooting Faith in a Mobile Culture

2010 First Printing

Copyright © 2010 by Jonathan Wilson-Hartgrove

ISBN: 978-1-55725-623-2

Unless otherwise noted, scriptural references are taken from the New Revised Standard Version Bible, copyright © 1989 by the Division of Christian Education of the National Council of the Churches of Christ in the United States of America, and are used by permission. All rights reserved.

Scriptural references marked KJV are taken from the Authorized King James Version of the Bible.

Library of Congress Cataloging-in-Publication Data
Wilson-Hartgrove, Jonathan, 1980-
The wisdom of stability : rooting faith in a mobile culture/by Jonathan Wilson-Hartgrove ; Foreword by Kathleen Norris.
    p. cm.
Includes bibliographical references (p.   ).
 ISBN 978-1-55725-623-2
1. Home—Religious aspects—Christianity. 2. Christian life—Baptist authors. 3. Vow of stability. I. Title. BR115.H56W55 2010
 248--dc22   2010000111

10 9 8 7 6 5 4 3 2 1

Published by Paraclete Press
Brewster, Massachusetts
www.paracletepress.com
Printed in the United States of America

For Dad,
who established roots of love in Stokes County's soil
and keeps bearing fruit.

CONTENTS

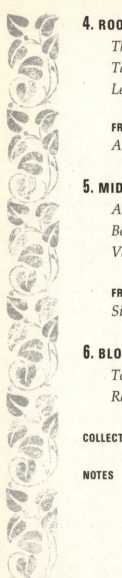

*I*t is brave of Jonathan Wilson-Hartgrove to tackle the subject of stability, when in American culture we learn early on to keep our options open, always ready for the new, improved model, the latest "best thing." We consider stability tedious at best. At its worst it is seen to restrict our freedom and limit our potential. For many of us, stability is an uneasy concept; we don't think about it much except to worry that if we remain in one place while the world changes around us we risk stagnating and becoming irrelevant. In a postmodern era of exponential change, how can we take stability seriously, let alone consider it a virtue?

In often surprising ways, this author forces stability from its cocoon of abstraction and dislodges our comfortable assumptions about it. He asks us to consider, among other things, the political and social implications of stability. Writing of the troubled neighborhood where he and his family have chosen to put down roots, Wilson-Hartgrove notes that its "problems . . . are directly connected to a culture where success means moving up and out. . . . The homelessness of guys who are hooked on crack . . . is but the flipside of the placelessness that drives ambitious young students to see this university town as a stop on their way to somewhere else." In a culture devoted to the pursuit of success and fame, what makes stability so unappealing may be that it acts as "the great leveler in a society of widening gaps, calling each of us, whatever our social status, to acknowledge the extent to which we're equally bound by powers beyond our control." What we most need, the author insists, is something that only stability can provide, "a way of life founded on solid ground, freeing us from the illusion that we can live without limits."

Stability might have remained an abstract concept for me had I not, much to my surprise and often against my better instincts, found myself in a marriage that lasted for nearly thirty years until my husband died. The wonderful insight of Wilson-Hartgrove's, that stability is not something we accomplish but is always a gift, resonates with my own experience. "The heart's true home," he writes, "is a life rooted in the love of God, but the Christian tradition insists that this love is always God's mercy directed at us *before* it is our response of trusting love. God offers us stability in the only thing that cannot fail—God's faithfulness itself" (emphasis mine). Sometimes the conviction that it is God who has brought two people—or a community—together is all we need to keep us in the struggle to nurture and maintain relationships of trust, respect, and love. Committing to such stability is never easy, but it is always worth a try.

Drawing on the 1700-year-old Christian tradition of monastic wisdom, the author reminds us that when we opt for stability we face a cosmic struggle. There are internal battles, of course, mostly with the demons of anger, pride, and boredom. But to commit to stability also means accepting other people as they are. How dreary to consider that God has given us this family, this spouse, these colleagues on the job, this church congregation. Surely we are meant for more important things, and our talents will be better appreciated by a more sophisticated crowd. Hitting on what he terms a "bedrock reality," Wilson-Hartgrove reminds us of the main reason Christianity will always remain unpalatable to those who are seeking an easy, ethereal spirituality. "Life with the God we know in Jesus Christ," he writes, "is lived in community with other people." Of course conflicts will come. Our job is to face them openly and honestly, and above all, to seek reconciliation. Stability is an essential in this process.

Seek is perhaps a dangerous word to use when discussing stability, because in some ways stability is the antithesis of the relentless seeking that is so prominent a part of American religious life. One of the more radical premises of this book is that there comes a time to set seeking aside. But as the romance of our initial religious experience fades, and the reality of life with other human beings in a church congregation seems too much to bear, we are tempted to move on. Wilson-Hartgrove asks us to stop a moment and ask if we might abandon our seeking, settle down, and allow God to find us where we are.

With its appealing mixture of personal experience and reflection along with lively biblical interpretation, this is a book in the tradition of Annie Dillard's *Pilgrim at Tinker Creek*, demonstrating the wealth of wisdom that can come when we commit ourselves, as Wilson-Hartgrove writes, "to a place and . . . watch it change before our eyes." Stability helps us to do the necessary foundation work so that we can pay close attention to what is going on around us, and adapt to changing conditions without losing our sense of place. Only stability can give us a way to accept the vicissitudes of life with a sense of peace, and even joy. It does not limit us but encloses us within God's love, so that with the psalmist we can say:

"The boundary lines have fallen for me in pleasant places;
I have a goodly heritage." (Psalm 16:6)

—KATHLEEN NORRIS
Honolulu, Hawaii

his is a book about staying put and paying attention. In a culture that is characterized by unprecedented mobility and speed, I am convinced that the most important thing most of us can do to grow spiritually is to stay in the place where we are. I am not advocating a stubborn provincialism or harking back to a time before the Internet and the automobile when "things were simpler" and "life was easier." Nor am I denying that God called Abraham, saying, "Go . . . " or that Jesus left his disciples with roughly the same marching orders. But I am convinced that both our use of new technologies and our faithful response to God's call depend on something more fundamental—a rootedness that most of us sense we are missing in our hurry to keep up amid constant change. I believe we need to recover the wisdom of stability.

Maybe this book is little more than a confession of my own need. I was raised in Christian churches by people who loved me well, charged to go out there and make a difference in the world, and given some of the best resources and training available for the task. I showed the *Jesus* film in the African bush, helped build schools for AIDS orphans, dug latrines in the Dominican Republic, played with kids from the barrios of Venezuela, built houses in Honduras, and tutored kids in Philadelphia's inner city. A citizen of God's kingdom, I tried to put my American passport to work for good in the world. But racking up all those frequent flyer miles for Jesus, I felt lonely. I wanted to share God's love with others, but wasn't sure where to experience it myself.

Hung over from all that travel, I stumbled into a little intentional community of Christians who were trying to love one another and their neighbors. It wasn't easy . . . and it showed. But I saw something compelling in that little group's experiment with faith: they had given themselves to God and one another in a particular place. They saw one another's junk, and they could talk about it. In all the ordinariness of everyday life, they knew what it meant to need forgiveness and to receive it. In short, they were learning to love one another. God's love became real for me in that place. I caught a glimpse of what I had been looking for.

Like the blind man who received his sight in the Gospels, I looked around to see my world again as if for the first time. I reread the Bible and saw in it God's plan to redeem the world through a gathered people. Paul's letters came alive to me as I imagined him leading a network of community organizers, convinced that they were part of the most important movement the world had ever known. When I turned to church history, I felt that same energy in monastic writings. Christians had a pretty mixed record when it came to living out the kingdom Jesus proclaimed, but the monastic movements seemed to have kept the dream alive. I fell in love with the desert mothers and fathers, with Benedict and Francis and Lady Julian and Teresa of Avila. Here was a movement of which I wanted to be a part.

And I was not alone. This God movement was a living tradition, and the gift I had glimpsed in one little community was alive and well in other places, albeit under the radar of mainstream Christianity. My wife, Leah, introduced me to that first community, beginning a journey that we've shared ever since. We traveled to Iraq together at the beginning of the second Gulf War, taking our cue from the example of Francis, who crossed the lines and sat with the Muslims during the fifth Crusade. In Iraq we met others on similar paths, representing a host of communities we had not known before. Inspired by the hospitality of Iraqis at a place called Rutba, we returned home to found a community called Rutba House in the Walltown neighborhood of Durham, North Carolina. We did not know at the time that *rutba* means "order" in Arabic. But we did sense already that we were caught up in a "new monasticism," guided by the same power that stirred the early church and all those witnesses through the centuries.

We did not know what we were doing when we started Rutba House. We only knew that we had seen a glimpse of what God's love looks like and that we had to respond. I do not write in praise of ignorance; I know too well the pain of our mistakes. But I also know that awareness of our ignorance sent us searching for fellow travelers and listening to ancient voices. Stumbling to find our way as a community, we happened upon the wisdom of stability.

In short, stability's wisdom insists that spiritual growth depends on human beings rooting ourselves in a place on earth with other creatures. Most modern (or postmodern) people get uncomfortable when talking about commitment and stability. We worry that vows like stability can be dangerous. I was relieved to learn from the monastic tradition that people who have promised stability also worry about its dangers. (If you're especially worried about the potential pitfalls of stability, you might want to read chapter 5 first.) Still, teachers ancient and contemporary challenged us to stay put. We have tried to listen to them. This book is an attempt to say what we have learned.

Staying, we all know, is not the norm in our mobile culture. A great deal of money is spent each day to create desires in each of us that can never be fulfilled. I suspect that much of our restlessness is a return on this investment. Mobility has a large marketing budget. While I don't imagine that I can outdo Madison Avenue, I do believe stability has a power to sell itself. If you bought this book, I hope you'll consider it a down payment on the fulfillment of your truest desire for wholeness. If you received it as a gift or borrowed it from a friend, all the better. The wisdom in these pages was all passed on to me free of charge. My work (which I've done the best I know how) was arranging the words.

Books like this one are written to persuade, and I'm of the conviction that an author ought to be frank about what he or she wants from a reader. So I'll say this from the start: I hope to reprogram your default setting. As participants in a mobile culture, our default is to move. God embraces our broken world, and I have no doubt that God can use our movement for good. But I am convinced that we lose something essential to our existence as creatures if we do not recognize our fundamental need for stability. Trees can be transplanted, often with magnificent results. But their default is to stay.

Should you ever leave the place where you are? I don't know. But I trust we are able to best discern the call of God in the company of friends when we are rooted in the life-giving wisdom of stability.

1

FOUNDATION WORK

The house I live in was built in 1910, when Walltown was just becoming a neighborhood.

It must have been a fine place then. Perched on a hill opposite the neighborhood church, its ten-foot ceilings with a second floor above would have exhibited spaciousness in stark contrast to the shotgun houses that lined most of these streets. In a place where black folks still accuse "uppity" neighbors of pretension by calling them "two-story Negroes," a house like this one sticks out. Someone decided to shoot the moon when they built this place.

But the house is old now, and it shows. We moved in just after a large extended family had finished using the place as a staging ground for their drug business. Such activity (and the lack of care that generally accompanies it) takes a toll on a place and its people. Most of the house's previous residents are gone now—buried, locked away in prison, or moved without a forwarding address. The house slouches like an old couch you might find at a yard sale—not finished, exactly, but irreparably marked by a history. The cracks in the plaster, mostly covered by caulking and paint now, suggest that the foundation is not precisely where it used to be. Over the years, things have shifted.

The instability I see in the walls of the structure I call home is troubling. They point me to foundation issues that need attention. But the cracked walls and crooked doorjambs also serve as a sign of the times, reminding me of the stability that all creation longs for in a culture of constant change. As long as the ground beneath us doesn't move, we humans tend to overlook the support structures that make life itself possible. But when we see a crack or, worse, feel a tremor, we're often dumbfounded. "When the foundations are being destroyed," the psalmist asks in a moment of desperation, "what can the righteous do?"

If these walls could talk, I can imagine them joining their voices with the psalmist. Together they might say to us, "Listen, we have some foundation issues that need attention."

By all accounts, we are living at the beginning of the twenty-first century in a time of unprecedented change. To get my head around just how much has changed in the past century, I sometimes think about my great-granny's life. Raised on a farm in southwest Virginia in the early 1900s, she refused to ever fly in an airplane, insisting that the only way one of those things was going to kill her was if it fell out of the sky and hit her on the head. In the relatively short span of the nine decades she lived through during the twentieth century, Granny saw the world transformed from a place where her mother sent her on a day's walk to carry chickens to market, to a world in which she watched her grandchildren go around the globe and back, sometimes within a week. Small wonder that she couldn't take it all in.

I think, too, about the change I have seen since Granny died. One summer in the late nineties, I spent a couple of months living with missionaries in rural Zimbabwe. While there, I wrote a letter to Granny and put it in the mail. My family joked that I almost beat the letter home.

Hardly more than a decade later, a normal day for me includes e-mailing a friend in Iraq, speaking with a coworker in Brazil via the Internet, and teleconferencing with people in six different time zones. Not only have we now collapsed the travel time between almost any two places in the world to less than a day, but also we have made it possible for anyone to be virtually anywhere almost any time. The speed at which all of this has happened is dizzying.

Most of the time we celebrate these advances, rightly noting the many ways they stimulate creativity and invigorate culture. To stop changing is to die, we note. We challenge ourselves to keep up with the latest in technology and push the limits of human potential. But constant shifting also takes its toll, as I'm reminded when I contemplate the cracks in the plaster of our old home. Foundations matter, these walls seem to say. Experts in their various fields are beginning to agree.

Take the ecologists, for example. They worry that the historically unprecedented change of the past hundred years has shaken the foundations of the environment that sustains human life. At the same time, many psychologists suggest that the multitasking of our information age is leading to a dangerous form of distraction, dulling the analytical functions of our brains that allow us to make good decisions. As I write in the midst of the global financial crisis that first hit headlines in 2008, the airwaves are filled with nearly constant commentary about fundamental economic uncertainty. Their fingers always on the pulse of our collective fears, marketing firms know we are desperate for something solid to hold on to. "What does over 100 years of *stability* bring to a relationship?" asks a quarter-page ad in the *New York Times*. "In today's ever-changing economy," it advises, "you need a bank you can trust."

Like children stumbling off a merry-go-round, Americans are grasping for something to anchor our lives in a sea of constant change. According to an Associated Press report from April 24, 2009, the number of Americans on the move has declined sharply in recent years, reaching the lowest percentage since the government began tracking mobility patterns just after the Second World War. Both recreational and business travel are down as families and businesses cut back to weather tough economic times.

Add to these trends the social movements—both conservative and progressive—that have emerged in response to a fundamental sense of uncertainty in our culture. From homeschool parents who want to keep their kids closer to their moral center, to the Slow Food movement that wants to shorten the distance between where food is grown and where it is eaten, people are beginning to stand their ground against the tides of mobility. "Staying is the new going," a friend quips. In the midst of the storm that rages about us, there is a movement toward stability.

But if there are trends leading us to question and even resist the more disastrous side effects of our hypermobile culture, they may only serve to confirm the degree to which we are desperately habituated in an unstable way of life. Even our movements to address the evident crisis, notes poet and agrarian Wendell Berry, almost always fail to be radical enough. "They deal with single issues or single solutions, as if to assure themselves that they will not be radical enough."

Though reactionary movements may be right in their analysis that something is broken and needs our attention, they fall short because they so often fail to address the root problem. They never get to the foundational issues, we might say. "The outward harmony that we desire between our economy and the world," writes Berry, "depends finally upon an inward harmony between our own hearts and the originating spirit that is the life of all creatures. . . . We can grow good wheat and make good bread only if we understand that we do not live by bread alone."

When I follow the cracks in my plaster to their source, I find a foundation beneath our house in need of repair. In a similar way, if we follow our longings for harmony and community to their root, we uncover a fundamental human need. Our desire for some place on earth to plant our feet in troubled times points us to the deeper yearnings of the human heart—to a spiritual need for stability that may well be built into us.

Whether you attribute this longing for stability to nature or nurture, it's hard to ignore its power, especially during those times in our personal and communal lives when we feel like we need something solid to hold on to. I know getting married triggered a nesting instinct in me, tempering my desire to travel the world and spurring me on toward some semblance of a real job. Ask any pastor in the United States when their church has been the most crowded since the turn of the millennium, and barring a tragedy that touched their specific community, the most likely answer is, "The Sunday after September 11, 2001." Whether we're facing a significant life change or a sudden tragedy, our instinct in times of change is to reach for something stable.

The great Wisdom Literature of almost every culture testifies to our need for stability. "Are you able to keep your wandering soul still and to insert it in unity and never to abandon this unity?" asked one of the sages of ancient China, Lao-tzu, in the seventh century BC. "Without passing your own door, you can know the world. Without looking through the window, you can see the road to heaven. The farther you go, the less you know." Deep down in our bones, we seem to know that rapid change and constant motion are hazards to our spiritual health. Humans long for the simplicity of a life that blossoms into its fullness by becoming rooted in a place. However much we test our limits, we hope the hidden ground beneath all things is solid as a rock.

If our contemporary culture does not readily acknowledge how perpetual motion can dumb down our souls, we do maintain at least the memory that a faithful journey will always lead us back to where we started from, opening our eyes to the potential of a place that we were not able to see before we left it. It takes a trip to Oz for Dorothy to say and say again, "There's no place like home." Even when it is reduced to sentimental nostalgia, the sentiment has power because our longings point us homeward.

For the Christian tradition, the heart's true home is a life rooted in the love of God. Like Lao-tzu and Dorothy both, Christian wisdom about stability points us toward the true peace that is possible when our spirits are stilled and our feet are planted in a place we know to be holy ground. When we get this stability of heart deep down inside of us, real growth begins to happen.

The trouble, all the saints insist, is that we cannot find stability within ourselves alone. The heart is like a vast ocean without a bottom. Seekers may plumb its depths and achieve incredible insight into the human condition. We may even, like a lifeboat adrift at sea, understand our desperate need for something solid to give us our bearings. But left to ourselves, we simply float. Without something greater than ourselves to ground our existence, our fragmented lives easily become like a grand old house on a poor foundation. No matter how good we are at covering the cracks, something fundamental is still missing.

The House of God

If stability is indeed a foundation for the life of faith, we might expect to learn something about what it looks like from the great fathers of our tradition. Jacob is right at the heart of the story of God's people. Indeed, he is the father from whom all the children of Israel descend. But if you were to search the scriptures and traditions of all the world's great religions, you'd be hard pressed to find a *worse* model of stability than Jacob.

In the Genesis account, Jacob flees his parents' home after he swindles his older brother, Esau, out of his birthright, first by exploiting Esau's hunger and taking his inheritance in exchange for a bowl of lentils, then by taking advantage of their father's blindness and stealing the blessing that was due to Esau as the firstborn son. Running for his life, Jacob is not sure where he's going next, only that he cannot stay home. A fugitive, he lies down on a stone under the cover of night to catch a little sleep before morning light.

This is when God intervenes in Jacob's story. In a dream, Jacob sees a ladder, planted firmly on earth, extending into heaven. Angels scurry up and down its rungs, bridging the divide between God and humanity. Beside where Jacob lies, if only for a few hours of stolen sleep, God stands with his feet on the ground to say, "the land on which you lie I will give to you and your offspring."

There it is: stability as pure gift. God meets Jacob when he is a homeless scoundrel on the run and says, "I love you. I want you. I will make this a place for you, and I will meet you here."

The heart's true home—the foundation we long for—is a life rooted in the love of God. But this love is always God's mercy directed toward us before it is our response of trusting love. God offers us stability in the only thing that cannot fail—God's faithfulness itself.

But the promise is not enough to make Jacob stay put. Come morning, he's on the road again. Still, Jacob cannot deny the importance of this place. "Surely the LORD is in this place—and I did not know it," Jacob exclaims on waking from his dream. "This is none other than the house of God," he exclaims, "and this is the gate of heaven."

Eventually Jacob will be called Israel—one who contends with God—because he doesn't settle down easily with the God who reaches out to him in love. As people whose impulses are shaped by an epoch of hypermobility, we may indeed find a true father in Jacob. We are, after all, a people on the run, propelled forward both by the ambition that keeps our eyes on the horizon and the broken relationships that we keep trying to leave behind. If God showed up where we stop to catch a breather in the midst of all this hurry, we too might be surprised. We do not, for the most part, have a sense that we stand on holy ground.

But God intervenes. Our race to the next thing is interrupted by an invitation to stay and dwell in the house of God. This is the incredible thing: despite the cracks that run like fault lines through our lives, pointing to a foundation in desperate need of repair, God meets us in the place where we are. In the midst of our spiritual strivings, when we know enough to know that something is wrong but do not have the capacity within ourselves to make it right, God shows up. Stability is indeed possible, *but only as a gift.*

The fractures in our lives and in our world suggest a problem at the very foundation of the world that we call home. At our best, we can see and name the ways the world around us is broken. We cry out against injustice, ache for community, and long for divisions to somehow be reconciled. We scramble for stability, even in a world of constant change, trying to shore up our foundations even as we stumble to stay on the run.

But however far we wander from the stability we were made for, children of Israel remember that our true home is in the house of God. The Psalms are replete with expressions of our longing to accept the invitation to come home to life with God. "I, through the abundance of your steadfast love, will enter your house," we say. The Twenty-third Psalm, famous for its assurance that God will take care of us, ends with the hope that "I shall dwell in the house of the LORD my whole life long." Indeed, the lowest place in the house of God is better than a life of apparent luxury lived somewhere else. "I would rather be a doorkeeper in the house of my God than live in the tents of wickedness."

The house of God is our greatest hope, the true home toward which all our strivings point us. Yet here it is in the foundation story of Israel, a gift offered to a wandering scoundrel. Stability does not depend on our ability to shore up crumbling foundations in the midst of change and confusion. Rather, it rests on the character of One who promises to love us where we are. Faith is a response to that love, rooting us in the reality of a God who is faithful.

A Way of Life with God

The practice of stability is the means by which God's house becomes our home. The word *home* comes from a root meaning "the place where one lies," an image that evokes the memory of Jacob lying on the dirt from which he had been made in the beginning, resting in the house of God even before he'd come to know it as his home. Without the gift of God's presence in the place where we are, stability is only an ideal for humans to aspire to—the unachievable goal of spirits whose reach must exceed their grasp. So the ground of stability is always God's grace. But the stability God invites us into is a practice that entails a way of life. To dwell in the house of God is to be transformed into people who know the ways and means of God.

The New Testament's epistle to the Ephesians says, "You are . . . members of the household of God, built upon the foundation of the apostles and prophets, with Christ Jesus himself as the chief cornerstone. In him the whole structure is joined together and grows into a holy temple unto the Lord; in whom you also are built together spiritually into a dwelling-place for God." In a world of constant change, we are given a firm foundation—a tradition of "apostles and prophets" who have rooted their lives in the life of God, with God in human flesh as the chief cornerstone. The promise of God's faithfulness is concrete—as real as people who have walked where we walk, stood where we stand, breathed the air that keeps us alive.

If the promise that grounds our stability is earthy, so too is the practice of living it out. We are "built together spiritually" in the words of Ephesians, but we ought not think that "spiritual" here suggests anything less concrete than the flesh-and-blood life of Jesus walking and talking with the apostles. Life in the house of God is life with other people who are every bit as broken and messed up as we are. We learn to dwell with God by learning the practices of hospitality, listening, forgiveness, and reconciliation—the daily tasks of life with other people. Stability in Christ is always stability in community.

Perhaps no one knows this better than those who promise themselves to a specific community of real people for life. The Trappist monk Thomas Merton wrote that "the real secret of monastic stability is, then, the total acceptance of God's plan by which the monk realizes himself to be inserted into the mystery of Christ through this particular family and no other." Monks vow stability when they join a community, living as visible signs of the truth Ephesians stresses for every person caught up in God's story: already made from the stuff of earth, we are being refashioned into a dwelling place for God, each of us supporting one another like bricks in a wall.

In Merton's words again, we have been "destined from all eternity to bring one another closer to [God] by our love, our patience, our forbearance, and our efforts at mutual understanding." We grow up into a life with God, built on a firm foundation, as we learn to dwell in a place with particular people. We take on the savor of God's love as we become one with the walls. In God's house, that means finding ourselves in one another.

Stability in Community

We find the stability we were made for as we come home to life with God in community with other people. This is our true home. But settling in isn't easy.

Will told me the story of relocating his family to be part of a church that takes community seriously. After a year in the new location, he met with one of his pastors to talk about how things were going. Life was good, Will reflected, and he was grateful for the welcome that he and his family had received at the new church. But he wasn't sure that he was experiencing the community he had expected. Frankly, Will had hoped for more.

The pastor listened to his misgivings, then asked how long Will and his family had been there. "About a year," he replied.

"Then I guess you've got about a year's worth of community," his pastor said matter-of-factly. "Stay another year and you'll have two years' worth. Stay thirty and you might find some of what you're looking for."

Our hunger for "community" may be the clearest contemporary expression of the heart's yearning for its true home. Despite cell phones and social networks that create the possibility for almost constant contact with the people we love, most of us feel alienated from our neighbors and unsure of where we belong. We ache with desire for true community, yet all of our social habits push us to seek what we're longing for somewhere else.

If we stand back and look at ourselves from a distance, we can see the paradox: the same restlessness that sends us searching for community also keeps us from settling down wherever we are. From a distance, it's almost funny. But when I'm actually living my life in real time, trying to pay attention to the person in front of me while fighting the temptation to think about the other things I might be doing if I weren't having this conversation, I'm not laughing. Instead, I feel as though I'm being subjected to the medieval torture of having a horse tied to each of my limbs and spurred to run in opposite directions.

In the midst of such turmoil, who wouldn't want a little stability? Like soldiers who've been on the front lines for back-to-back tours, we are sensitized to our basic human desire for stability by the extreme lack of it in a hypermobile culture. But in an economy of limitless growth that depends on the continual creation of unfulfilled desire, stability's wisdom, like anything else, can be reduced to a commodity that does not satisfy the spirit but only sends us rushing off in search of greater insight and understanding somewhere else. At best, our deepest longings point us homeward. But desire alone does not make a home. Stability demands that we do the long, hard work of life with other people in the place where we are.

A community of Benedictines I know is encouraged by the significant increase in visitors coming for retreat in recent years. To accommodate them all, they've had to build a large new guest house. But they are also aware of the danger that a weekend with the monks can become an experience that people purchase to satisfy a spiritual itch without having to seriously rethink how they live with the people in their parish or on their cul-de-sac. True stability can never be a product for individuals to consume. Rather, it is an invitation to shared life with particular people in a specific place.

Writing about stability as lifelong promise in monastic community, Michael Casey says it "cannot be realized without spending a substantial part of one's life and investing one's energies within monastery limits, living in a state of mutual visibility with others in the community." This isn't just the case for monks. All stability challenges us to engage the people where we are. We do not listen to monastic wisdom but rather exploit it if we believe that we can enjoy the life with God that it points to without engaging this bedrock reality: life with the God we know in Jesus Christ is lived in community with other people. We can only grow into the fullness of what we are made to be in Christ by opening ourselves to the particular brothers and sisters who mediate Christ's presence to us.

Despite our longing for community, we often hide from a "state of mutual visibility with others" because it is more difficult than cultivating a personal spirituality and sense of tranquility. This is at least part of the reason books on spirituality have become more popular in the last generation, even as church attendance has gone down significantly. Choosing a spirituality that works for me is so much easier than dealing with the people who show up at the church in my neighborhood.

The trouble, though, is that a spirituality that works for me cannot save me. Satisfied by an idea of God that makes me feel better, I'm left alone, without the support that comes from being built into a wall of shared life that rests on the foundation of the God who has been our dwelling place in every generation.

But if this problem is larger than me—if it is a cultural problem, bound up with our economy and as concrete as technology—what difference does it make for me to try to stay somewhere and find community? Commit yourself to a place and you will watch it change before your eyes. Promise yourself to a church or a neighborhood and its people will move on. Stability can begin to sound like wishful thinking, especially when we feel burned by people who decide to move on. Maybe we have to be realistic. Times change, after all.

The biblical image of a gathered community as the house of God may have made sense in the ancient world, but it hardly seems plausible today. Shouldn't we try to reimagine the gospel for a postmodern culture? Couldn't we find the stability we're looking for by inviting God to dwell in our hearts or to inhabit the space at the center of our social networks? Lest we give up hope entirely, we may be tempted to reconceive the practice of stability as something "spiritual" that doesn't challenge our bodies to actually stay in one place. We do it for the best of reasons. But I suspect we lose something of stability's power when we reduce it to something realistic.

When Clarence Jordan learned the New Testament concept of *koinonia* at a Southern Baptist seminary in the 1930s, it seemed incredible to him that the Scriptures white Christians revered would contain within them a concept so contrary to the racial divisions of the South. How could white and black people have fellowship with one another and be built up into a dwelling place for God in a place where it was illegal to eat together in a restaurant? Jordan was compelled by the somewhat unrealistic promise that God wanted to live among people in such a partnership. Together with his family and a few friends, he started an interracial community called Koinonia Farm in southwest Georgia.

Nearly two decades later, when the community became a natural place for civil rights workers to stop for rest and planning meetings, the Ku Klux Klan caught on to what people at Koinonia Farm were about and started trying to get rid of them. Boycotts against their produce nearly stamped out the life of the farm, and the community seriously considered whether it was time to move somewhere else. But Jordan insisted they were called to stay. Reflecting on the relationship between the community and the piece of land they inhabited, he said that when "men say to you, 'Why don't you sell it and move away?' they might as well ask, 'Why don't you sell your mother?' Somehow God has made us out of this old soil and we go back to it and we never lose its claim on us. It isn't a simple matter to leave it."

Committed to stability throughout the turbulent 1950s and '60s, Koinonia Farm endured an economic boycott, firebombs, and gunshots into their homes. Staying was not easy. But in a 1966 letter to his son, Jordan summed up the faith that grounded his commitment to stay. "This is what always baffles me. Koinonia is forever dying and forever living. We should have conked out long ago, but somehow others came in the nick of time. This half-born condition is agonizing, and I could wish it otherwise, but there it is."

Stability in community is always a half-born condition. We are suspended between heaven and earth on a ladder that promises communion with God but is also planted firmly on the ground. To both see clearly the life we are made for and, at the same time, to have to deal with the selfish desires and petty preferences of people where we are is, indeed, agonizing. "But there it is," Jordan says with a different kind of realism. Stability is a commitment to trust God not in an ideal world, but in the battered and bruised world we know. If real life with God can happen anywhere at all, then it can happen here among the people whose troubles are already evident to us.

Community is always a risk. We cannot know beforehand who will stay and who will leave. But each decision to stay—every prayer lifted up from our half-born condition—can be seen as an act of faith that our God will give us what we need, as Clarence Jordan said, "in the nick of time." To trust the God of Jacob is to know that God is in this place, whether we sense yet that the place is holy or not. My well-being is tied up with the health of my neighbor—even my enemy—and the place on earth that we share. No, we cannot halt the tide of mobility through a stubborn insistence to stand our ground. We can, however, trust that our God is a firm foundation, giving us grace to stand even when it seems we will all be swept away. We can entrust ourselves to one another in faith.

Dorothy Bass, a Lutheran theologian from the Midwest, tells a story about a church she grew up in. Her father was an elder in the church, and she remembers how he agreed to chair the fundraising committee for a new education building, even though he knew their family would be moving before the building was finished. Looking back, she said she could see how her father's determination to sit through meetings, count pledge cards, and deal with the arguments that every church has about money was grounded in his love for the people of that church. He wanted the life of faith to flourish in that place, so he did the hard work of building a space for life together to happen. "We didn't stay in the town," Bass says, "but I believe my father practiced stability by serving that church as if he would never leave it."

Maybe every attempt to keep faith with people wherever we are is a subversion of the spirit of the age. When Jacob rose in the early morning after his ladder vision, the story says he paused before continuing his flight. Jacob picked up the stone he had slept on, planted it upright in the ground, and prayed to the God who had interrupted his sleep. If God would spare him, Jacob said, and let him return home in peace, then this stone of remembrance would be called Beth-el—that is, the house of God.

Jacob kept running—and we keep moving too—but in time he came back to that place. God met him again at Bethel and gave him his new name, Israel. Out of a fugitive, God created a placed people. Scattered and divided though we children of Jacob may be, our story still calls us to remember that the place where we lie is holy ground. The house of God is as close to us as the people whom we eat and argue with, and it can become our home, a foundation for the life of faith, if we trust God to sustain us in community. That it will be a struggle is assumed from the start. Israel means "the one who wrestles with God." But getting down to the business of wrestling with the One who made us is a big step toward addressing our most fundamental need. It is the foundation work all our struggles point us toward, the starting place each of us needs.

Bird Watching

My son JaiMichael, who doesn't want me to scare the bird, says to be quiet before I walk onto the front porch. He is watching through the storm door, studying the work of this busy homemaker. She is perched on the top of our open mailbox, trying to maneuver a leaf clutched in her beak. Later, after she has flown away and JaiMichael lets me out the door, I look in the mailbox to see the beginnings of a nest, fashioned since I brought in yesterday's mail. From the stuff of earth, a mother bird scrambles to make a home. Nature's instinct is grounded, even for those with wings.

I notice beneath my feet floorboards that were mended last week. They are not yet painted gray like the boards around them—boards that I walk across thirty times a day. They are fresh-cut pine. Seeing their grain exposed, I remember I'm standing on trees. I am surrounded by a forest, cut and refashioned by hands more precise than a beak, but no less dependent. I do not know enough to make a home with my own two hands, but I am inextricably bound up with people who do. By the work of our hands and the grace that enlivens them, we are all busy homemakers.

But how easy it is to forget the wood beneath my feet, the hands that make a home, the fragility of every nest, the spirit's need for a place on earth. God is everywhere, it's true. But I am not. I am tied to a place, dependent on its people. I am counting on the pine boards beneath my feet, and on Jeff who nailed them there last week. This is a fragile nest, and I am a bird.

JaiMichael calls from inside to tell me he is hungry. I walk to the kitchen, empty the contents of an instant oatmeal packet, and add the milk and water. When we have eaten, we walk across the porch, down the front yard, and around the corner to say morning prayer with brothers and sisters in our community. I read a psalm: "My heart is firmly fixed, O God, my heart is fixed."

Walking home, I sing a song I've learned to love at the church across the street from our house. "Woke up this mornin' with my mind stayed on Jesus. . . . " Truth is, though, I didn't wake up with my heart fixed or my mind stayed. I was distracted by the day's to-do list, an exchange from yesterday that annoyed me, unrealistic hopes for what I might get done today if I just got started a little early—and all of this before breakfast.

Stability of heart does not come naturally. But the simple rhythms of tending to body and soul—making oatmeal and saying prayers, keeping house and singing songs—bring me back to a center, to a still point that is fixed in this place. I do not know how to eliminate distractions (even if I shut down my e-mail, turn off the cell phone, and drive to a pristine retreat center, my thoughts are still with me).

But I can keep the rhythms that are given to me by my church and community. I can listen to my

son and watch the birds more closely. The desert mother Amma Syncletica said, "If a bird abandons the eggs she has been sitting on, she prevents them from hatching, and in the same way monks or nuns will grow cold and their faith will perish if they go around from one place to another." I hold this fragment like a leaf in my beak. I'll take what I'm given and build with it.

2

A PLACE TO BEGIN

*I*t is summer in Walltown. If I get up early enough to sit on our front porch before the day's duties demand my attention, there is a hint of coolness in the damp air. I breathe in the thick, dark smell of soil and shade, made pungent by last night's thundershower. The neighborhood is quiet enough for me to hear robins scurry between the branches of the sprawling pecan tree in our front yard. In the distance, about half a mile away, I can hear the rumble of eighteen-wheelers traveling north and south on I-85. I sit in a rocking chair and survey our block by early morning's light. "The LORD is in his holy temple; let all the earth keep silence before him." When I sit still and pay attention, I can see that this is holy ground.

But this is not easy to remember. By eight in the morning the sun is beckoning last night's rain back up into the heavens. I begin the day's work swimming through humid air—what a friend and I called "instant sweat" when we were growing up in North Carolina's tobacco country, not far from here. In the western mountains of our state, this summer haze turns the ridges blue, and tourists come to enjoy the sight. Down here in the Piedmont, we just endure the humidity.

Southerners invented sweet tea as fuel for our march through the waters of summer. But caffeine and cane sugar were not sufficient comfort for a people who despised the toil of wrestling life from a land soaked in humidity. Giving in to our baser instincts, we cursed the ground our ancestors had stolen from the Cherokee and the Choctaw, the Lumbee and the Creek. Those who had power forced men and women with black skin to do the dirty work of priming tobacco and picking cotton. Those who didn't turned from sweet tea to stronger drink, drowning sorrow and sickness in the sweet medicine called moonshine.

This aversion to soil and toil has shaped our economic and religious lives alike. By and large, the God we learned to worship in this place eased our spirits (like good moonshine) and promised a better home in heaven in the sweet by and by. More than a few people have noted how the Southern way of life tried to drive a wedge between the spirit and the body, entangling us in a terrible web of racism, environmental degradation, and other-worldly spirituality. But standing on my front porch, surveying a neighborhood that has both suffered and survived this death-bound system, I cannot help noticing how our spiritual struggle is inextricably tied to this place—its heat and humidity, its highways and horticulture. Our demons are the same that people have faced throughout human history—greed, lust, envy, anger, acedia, love of money, vainglory, and pride. But both our evil thoughts and our responses to them have been shaped by the geography of this place. When our demons beckon us, they speak with a Southern drawl.

For better or worse, this is the modern wilderness where I've tried to stay put and do battle with the devil. God interrupted me when I was fleeing home, calling me back to find a foundation on the soil from which I'd grown. North Carolina is a far cry from the ancient Egyptian desert, but the spiritual mothers and fathers of that arid land have become guides to me as I've learned to practice stability in this place.

The desert monastics of the third and fourth centuries were not sure how to live faithfully as both citizens of heaven and citizens of the Roman Empire, but they knew they could not find their way by running from the root of temptation, which they located in their own hearts. Led by Abba Antony, they went into their cells and stayed for the purpose of doing battle with the demons of their day.

Someone asked Abba Antony, "What must one do in order to please God?" After encouraging the pilgrim to keep God before his eyes and pattern his life after the Scriptures, Antony added, "In whatever place you find yourself, do not easily leave it." Another of the desert fathers advised similarly, "If a trial comes upon you in the place where you live, do not leave that place when the trial comes. Wherever you go, you will find that what you are running from is ahead of you."

The wisdom of the desert was not my instinct. I grew up in King, North Carolina, and soon learned that I was from a humble place. Education opened my eyes to the problems of the place I was from and charged my imagination with a fascination for the landscape beyond King's horizons. I wanted to make a difference in the world, and I knew that meant leaving home. The way up to a higher calling was a highway that led out into the wide world of important places. I left home at sixteen, not looking back.

But the pursuit of higher truth in better places was frustrating. God is everywhere, for sure, but somewhere along the way I started to realize that highways are lonely and airports lack community. I wanted to love my neighbor, but I had not stayed in one place long enough to know my neighbors or my neighborhood. Tossed about by the tides of perpetual motion, I started looking for some place to drop my anchor. When I did, I found myself drawn toward home—to the soil of this Christ-haunted South where the demons I'd left to overcome still show up every Sunday morning for church.

Interrupted by Jesus

My own call to stability came when I was interrupted by the Jesus I thought I was trying to follow. Luke tells a story that challenged most of my assumptions about how God wanted me to make a difference in our world. After roughly thirty years in a small Galilean town, Jesus gets baptized by his cousin John, announces a jubilee campaign at his hometown synagogue, drafts a group of disciples to join his movement, heals a number of people, and tells some memorable parables. Jesus is as eager to make a difference as I ever was, and he does not mince words about the severity of society's problems.

But right in the middle of the story, just as Jesus' movement is picking up momentum, he tells a man *not* to follow him. This struck me as odd the first time I noticed it.

The man is naked when Jesus meets him. Stripped bare, his spiritual torment is unveiled for all to see. He is alone— without family, community, or the institutions of love that humans need to flourish. His life fragmented by the pull of myriad desires, this man is driven by a superhuman power into a frenzy of activity. Some have tried to bind him with chains, but he has broken free and fled. Ultimately, this man's running has landed him in the graveyard, living among the dead. He is, you might say, a manifestation of the struggle deep in the heart of the modern soul. He embodies our deepest fears of loneliness, disconnection, fragmentation, and death.

Jesus knows that, even in his condition, this demon-possessed man still has the potential to enjoy the life for which he was made. Jesus commands the demons to come out of him and go into a herd of pigs. Filled with the demons that had tormented the man, the pigs run off a cliff and into the lake. The point is clear enough: whatever just came out of this man is a force that will run living creatures to their death.

When the townspeople turn back from watching the pigs splash into the lake, they see the man who had been possessed "sitting at the feet of Jesus, clothed and in his right mind." No longer constantly driven to flee, this man has been healed. He is seated at the feet of the One who stands immovable. It's an incredible contrast to the scene when Jesus first set foot on the shore and the man came running, every muscle tense. Restless and distraught before, he is now seated, in his right mind. In the psychological language of our modern world, we might call him "stable."

Yet the sight of this man seated at Jesus' feet puts fear in the people of the town. We are, after all, accustomed to our demons. Despite our frustration and occasional acts of resistance, we accommodate ourselves to the ways they limit our own lives and crush the lives of others. However terrible our demons may appear when we look them in the face, their presence along the periphery of our lives feels normal. Maybe the demons kill, but we're often more comfortable with the frenetic forces that drive us here and there than we are with the radical new way of life that Jesus brings.

The people of this little town on the other side of the lake ask Jesus to leave. Respecting their wishes, he does. But as Jesus is getting into the boat, the man who has been made whole begs to go with Jesus. His peaceful posture is disturbed by the thought of Jesus leaving. For the first time in years, he has found peace with Jesus. Like a good disciple, he wants to sit at Jesus' feet. Indeed, he wants to follow Jesus' feet wherever they go.

But Jesus says no. "Return to your home, and declare how much God has done for you." Stay where you are. In whatever place you find yourself, do not easily leave it. Jesus delivers the demon-possessed man and then offers him the gift of stability. Maybe the single most important thing we can do if we want to grow spiritually is to stay in the place where we are.

This is a hard word for disciples who are eager to follow Jesus anywhere, so long as we don't have to stay put. When Jesus calls them to discipleship, Peter, James, and John leave their fishing nets. Levi leaves his tax booth. These disciples hit the road with Jesus, following in his footsteps to hang on his every word and learn the way that leads to life. In some ways, reading the gospel story is like going on that journey ourselves. We hear Jesus' promise of something new and are invited to follow with the disciples.

But in the face of demons who threaten to destroy life, Jesus says something we don't expect. *"Don't* follow me," Jesus says to one who had been driven in a multitude of directions by desires and impulses that no one could restrain. Do not flee to the promise of spiritual growth far away on the other shore. The same power that healed you can sustain a life of faithfulness right where you are. Do you believe that God can meet you here? Can you trust Jesus enough to stay?

These were the questions that brought me home to Southern soil. By the time I heard them clearly, I was not answering them alone. My wife, Leah, and I had traveled to my hometown on a winter break in college to commit to one another before God and family, trusting that we could follow Jesus better together than we could on our own. In the community of marriage, we found stability that was life-giving. But wrestling with issues of poverty, racism, and violence in inner-city Philadelphia, we learned that our battle was "not against flesh and blood," as Paul once wrote, but "against principalities and powers." They were the same powers I'd left home to struggle against—demons we sensed we would have to stay put to face. Taking a cue from the desert mothers and fathers, we looked for a wilderness on America's urban landscape where we could wrestle the demons that held us and the people we loved captive. We moved to Walltown and said we would not easily leave it.

The Ladder We Climb

Practicing stability has meant unlearning the habits of a culture that tells us the answer to our problems is always somewhere else. For most young people in the West, "good education" leads to a migratory existence. Conventional wisdom among the middle class says, "Go away from home for a good four-year degree. Go somewhere else for a master's. Travel around and see the world a little. Then maybe think about a terminal degree somewhere else." Even on the fast track, this plan will take you into your midthirties. By then, of course, we're well prepared for an economy that tells us where it needs us most. We sometimes call this "climbing the ladder," but even as a metaphor, it's a stretch. Without a stable foundation to rest on, ladders become dizzying and dangerous.

I had a neighbor growing up, Alan, who worked for the power company. He was a young guy then and didn't mind danger or odd hours, so the company put him on call for emergency repair jobs. Early one morning, Alan was called out to fix a stoplight at a busy intersection. He parked his ladder truck in the middle of the intersection, put out his caution cones, and climbed to fix the light, some twenty feet in the air. While he was working, a drunk driver raced through the intersection and clipped the back of Alan's truck. Alan flew off the top of his ladder, cut a back flip in the air, and somehow landed on his feet in the intersection. Miraculously, he wasn't hurt. But Alan had a hard time trusting ladders after that. Wanting to keep his feet on the ground, Alan found another job.

Most of us don't have an experience as jolting as Alan's, but his story may serve as something of a parable for our spiritual lives in a mobile culture. Even if we don't feel it now, we can remember a time when we felt young, confident, and ready to take on the world. We set out to excel and make a difference—to end poverty or fix a broken school system; to be the first college graduate in our family or the first black doctor in our town. If we were at all religious, we probably had some sense that these dreams were from God. We trusted the Lord to give us strength to go on when the journey seemed impossible. We were spurred on by the testimonies of those who had "made it," getting to the top of the ladder and achieving what they dreamed for so long.

Like Alan, though, we have felt the ground beneath the ladder shift from time to time. Maybe we saw it coming—a move to a new school, an internship in a new city, a long-hoped-for marriage to someone half a world away. Or maybe, like Alan, it blindsided us—a company transfer, a slouch in the economy, a sudden divorce. Whether as a result of carefully laid plans or catastrophic interruptions, few of us seem able to stay in one place anymore. Maybe we have survived the moves. (In some cases, our survival seems almost as miraculous as Alan's.) We're still alive, but our spirits are hungry. We long for connection with God and other people. We're desperate for community. We're hungry for a way to live that feels authentic and true.

Early in the sixth century, Benedict of Nursia summed up much of the desert tradition's wisdom and wrote a rule of life for monks who were longing for community and connection with God. Fifteen hundred years later, the *Rule of Benedict* is one of the most lasting and widespread guides for religious life in the West. Benedict knew that the spiritual seekers of his own day had big dreams and great hopes, not unlike the inner stirrings that had inspired his spiritual journey as a young man. Benedict did not squash human ambition, but he saw clearly that if we want to ascend to life with God, it matters a great deal which ladder we climb. Harkening back to Jacob, he wrote that "if we desire to attain speedily that exaltation in heaven to which we climb . . . then by our ascending actions we must set up the ladder on which Jacob in a dream saw angels descending and ascending."

Benedict did not affirm the pursuit of any and every dream. Like the African-American spiritual written a millennium later, Benedict insisted, "We are climbing *Jacob's* ladder." The angels going up and down from heaven to earth presented a practical lesson for Benedict's community: "Without doubt, this descent and ascent can signify only that we descend by exaltation and ascend by humility." The way that leads to life, Benedict told his followers, is a way of humility.

According to the Rule, people who follow this way of humility promise "stability, fidelity to monastic life, and obedience." The threefold commitment is made as one promise, Benedictines say, something like the Father, Son, and Holy Spirit are said to be one essence in Christian theology. But it's striking to me that Benedict decided to put stability first in his list. If we're going to climb Jacob's ladder toward the humility of Jesus, Benedictine wisdom says the first thing we need is a stable place to begin.

The humility we aspire to at our very best is inseparable from the humus beneath our feet—the ground that someone must till if we are to eat, that someone must tend if we are to survive. Stability of place begins with the humble acknowledgment that our life depends on the land we live upon. Barbara Kingsolver, one of our most articulate contemporary advocates for the land, reflects on her adult life, noting that she has dug asparagus beds into the yards of every house she has owned and some that she has rented. Why bother? we might ask, when asparagus is readily available at any good supermarket, and for much less trouble? Kingsolver answers, "I suppose in those unsettled years I was aspiring to a stability I couldn't yet purchase."

The trouble for most of us isn't so much that we cannot afford stability as it is that we don't value it. We idealize and aspire to a life on the move, spending what resources we have on acquiring skills that make us more market-able (that is, more mobile). We want to "move up in the world," which almost always means closer to a highway, an airport, or a shopping mall. I cannot deny that this is why I left the rural farming community where I grew up. But neither can I ignore the fact that this is what has been unraveling the neighborhood where I now live since the late 1960s.

Walltown, a historically black neighborhood, was a tight-knit extended family that fought to survive the racism of the Jim Crow South for much of the twentieth century. With the access that was gained through the civil rights movement, however, everyone who could leave Walltown did. The neighborhood was left to people without resources and became a prime stag-ing ground for the crack epidemic that hit Durham like a Mack truck in the 1980s.

The simile from interstate commerce is fitting because none of this would have been possible without I-85. A principal artery linking the major population centers of the Southeast, this highway made possible a mobility that was unimaginable a century before. By virtue of this new highway, Atlanta and Washington, DC, were suddenly a day's commute from one another. For an individual with an automobile and a tank of gas, the road was free.

The social cost of the interstate highway system, however, was carried disproportionately by poor African-American communities like Walltown and farmlands like the place where I was raised. In Wendell Berry's memorable phrase, "It made distant what had been close, and close what had been distant." Neighborhoods like Walltown that had already lost their educated and well-employed citizens were systematically cut off from the local economy by highways that made the next city closer than the other side of town. In such a situation, getting drugs from the highway and selling them to your neighbor came to look more like economic common sense than like self-destruction.

The summer Leah and I moved to Walltown, I heard gunshots through the open window in our bathroom as I was getting ready for bed one Saturday night. Such a sound was common enough that it did not interrupt my routine. I turned on a fan in our bedroom—both for the breeze and the background noise—and I went to sleep.

"The dogs howled all night long," Ms. Carolyn told me the next day as I stood on her front porch and watched the police come and go. They found Lil' Robert facedown in the drainage ditch behind the duplex that Ms. Dot and Ms. Nora shared. Standing at the intersection three doors down from our house, Robert had been hit in a drive-by shooting and left for dead by his friends. The news reported that he was a victim of gang violence, gunned down by rivals who felt he was infringing on their market share. What they didn't say was that the "competition" looked like him. They were his neighbors; victims, like him, of powers that insist nothing good could happen in a place like this.

In the face of such death-dealing violence, Jesus' words to the demon-possessed man are an invitation to be born again. The problems of neighborhoods like Walltown are directly connected to a culture where success means moving up and out, and education equals climbing the ladder in order to rise above common places. The homelessness of guys who are hooked on crack in Walltown is but the flipside of the placelessness that drives ambitious young students to see this university town as a stop on their way to somewhere else.

Perhaps stability is the great leveler in a society of widening gaps, calling each of us, whatever our social status, to acknowledge the extent to which we're equally bound by powers beyond our control. Rich or poor, we are in desperate need of the ladder that Benedict offers—a way of life founded on solid ground, freeing us from the illusion that we can live without limits and climb above the ground from which we were made.

A Spirituality for Staying Put

The image of a ladder recurs through the centuries of stability's wisdom, reminding us both of our need for a stable place to begin and of the distance we still need to cross. Finding a place on earth is not the end of our spiritual strivings, but rather a beginning. Having found a place to begin, we still need guidance to do well the work of staying.

Don lived for years in the Chicago area, working hard and trying to keep up with the fast pace of his profession. Several years ago, he left the city and took a job on a somewhat remote college campus run by Benedictines. While visiting on the campus once, he and I walked the carefully cared-for grounds, talking about our faith. "Since coming here," Don said, "I've given up my spiritual journey."

I could tell from his smile that he had a point to make, so I asked what he meant. "Well, you know, we Christians talk a lot about our spiritual journeys. We get excited about experiences and go places looking for the next spiritual high. We say God called us here. Then God calls us there. But it's all so individualistic. It's all so focused on little 'lessons' or 'insights' that we're supposed to take with us to the next place." Don paused and looked around at some of the old men in long black robes who were walking by us on the campus. "I think I'm learning from these guys that God can change us if we'll settle down in one place. So I've given up my spiritual journey. I'm going to just stay with God here and see how I can grow."

We cannot ignore the many ways that our culture of hypermobility has shaped how we think about our spiritual lives. Thanks to cheap plane tickets and strong economies, Christians in the West can go more places now than we've ever been able to go before. We go to Italy to see where Francis lived and to Ireland to learn about Celtic Christianity.

When it's relatively safe, we go to Israel to walk where Jesus walked. We go to conferences to hear from the latest spiritual gurus and we go to retreat centers to find some solace in our busy lives.

Of course, we find some good in all these places. But picking up fragments of spiritual wisdom can begin to feel like trying to piece together a tree from limbs that we've broken off here and there. Even if we gather enough limbs to make a tree, something is still missing. Life just isn't in the pieces the same way it is in a tree whose roots are fixed in the soil of a particular place.

Benedictine spirituality helps me piece together the fragments of my own spiritual journey for the sake of making progress in the place where I am. The twelfth-century Benedictine Bernard of Clairvaux names the challenge I face, having committed myself to stability. "I climb slowly, a weary traveler, and I need somewhere to rest," Bernard confesses. "Woe is me if the darkness surrounds me, or if I should flee in the winter or on the Sabbath, for now even at an acceptable time and in a day of salvation, I can scarcely make my way."

Stability doesn't make the spiritual life easy. Having given myself to Walltown, I've not seen it transformed before my eyes. The power of death is real in this place, and I often feel overwhelmed. Working to save a few kids from the grip of gangs, I'm driven to despair by a fledgling budget, frustrated by the kids' despondence, overwhelmed by my own anger at the sight of lives cut short before they ever really got started. Yes, I'm tempted to leave. Some days I don't know what faith means for me in this place, even less how to share it with someone else.

I find it reassuring on my worst days that Bernard and others like him, committed though they were to stability, still felt the temptation to flee. Having made the commitment to climb Jacob's ladder in a particular place, Benedictines have had to develop a spirituality of dynamic stability, naming the growth that is needed as we stay put. For Bernard, the struggle to make progress forced him to plunge deeper into Jacob's story. "It was better for Jacob when the sinew of his thigh shriveled at the touch of the angel, than for it to swell, collapse, and fall at the touch of the angel of pride," Bernard noted. "Would that the angel would touch my sinew and make it shrink, if as a result of this weakness I was able to progress. For I can make no progress in my own strength." Whatever progress we make on this way of humility is growth in our awareness of our own insufficiency. I cannot do anything—not even keep my own faith—alone.

I remember the pain of my neighbors who never had the option of leaving Walltown, but nevertheless learned to sing, "I told Satan / Get thee behind / Victory today is mine." Living and singing alongside them, I am learning that the victory I claim is not a celebration of my ability to overcome. Rather, it is a confession of my utter dependence on a power beyond me to progress toward abundant life in *this* place. On my best days, it is the faith I long for. But it is not easy. I need a community around me and the wisdom of a communion of saints across time to keep my feet on the ground.

William of Saint Thierry, a student of Bernard's in the twelfth century, noted that "every wise climber must know that the stages of ascent are not like the rungs of a ladder." To climb ever closer to God is not to move away from our troubled and troubling neighbors, but closer to them. For a people who struggle to stay put and make progress, Jacob's ladder might be best imagined as a bridge laid flat between divided people—a type of rebar, even, to support us as we are being built together into a community of faith.

Whether we think we have options or not, the wisdom of stability suggests that we can only begin to grow spiritually by accepting the gift of faith in the place where we are. We choose neither to flee to a better place on earth nor to despair in the face of demons that taunt us where we are. By God's grace, we stand and sing, "Just like a tree planted by the waters / I shall not be moved."

This refusal to flee is not a denial of our need for conversion but a confession of the renewal we always need. We are, after all, a pilgrim people on a journey toward our true home. We are Abraham's children, called to go to a land that God will show us. We are Israel in Egypt, trusting God to lead us out of bondage, through the waters, and into the Promised Land. We are disciples of the resurrected Jesus, hearing once again that he is going ahead of us into Galilee. Like the first disciples, we must follow after him. We *are* on a journey, marching up the King's highway, climbing Jacob's ladder to a building not made by hands.

But progress along this way is impossible, Benedictine wisdom insists, if we are not grounded in reality, planted by streams of living water, standing on the promises of the One who is our rock. Stability challenges us to question the assumptions of a hypermobile culture, but it ought not make us immovable. Staying put and paying attention are, rather, dynamic disciplines aimed at helping us grow and progress toward wholeness. "Monastic theologians interiorized the Christian custom of pilgrimage," writes contemporary Benedictine Charles Cummings. "Without leaving their abbeys, monks and nuns could leave all self-ish ways and go on an interior pilgrimage. . . . Stability became a broader, richer reality as it incorporated both the essence of pilgrimage and the essence of rootedness."

Here, then, is the spirituality I need to stay put: a ladder that brings together my need for a firm foundation and my need to progress toward holiness. For people who think little of flying across a continent, the assumption of Benedictine spirituality is striking: if we want our very being to rise up into God's being, nothing is more important than rooting ourselves in a place where God can happen. Yes, we're on a journey. But not all movement is progress toward the Promised Land (Israel wandered in the wilderness for forty years, after all). The difference between progress and wandering seems to depend on whether we can trust God to deliver us from bondage in the place where we are.

From the church parking lot across the street, I hear the voice of a young man from Walltown. He is yelling instructions to neighborhood kids who are playing outside during the first week of summer camp. I remember our first summer here, when that same young man was himself a kid in the camp and I was his counselor, trying to survive the humidity on blacktop in July. We were strangers then. I stayed, and we became friends. He came to live with our family, graduated from high school, and went off to college—not the norm around here. In the fall of his sophomore year, he told me he wanted to major in education and teach elementary school in the inner city. "Little black boys don't have many men to look up to," he said.

I watch out the window as the campers stand at attention, ready to jump at his command. "Maybe here," I think to myself, "they do."

Bare Feet

Greg sits beside me in a rocking chair, changing his socks and telling stories about the neighborhood. When you're homeless it's important to take care of your feet. When you belong to a place, its stories are in you.

I remember the stories Darryl told me about Greg—stories about the days when Greg was a track star at Hillside High School. "He was the fastest runner I ever seen," Darryl said, shifting his weight on his own sore feet. He and Greg had run the streets together until Darryl got religion, sobered up, and slowed down his life. It happened too late to save Darryl from his diabetes. Gangrene got in his feet—was already in them, I believe, that day he stood in the street telling stories about Greg. The doctors ended up taking Darryl's feet first, then his legs, before the gangrene finally took his life.

As for Greg, he's still running. He gets up early, both to catch breakfast at the Episcopal church and to keep from getting caught on the porch where he lay down for the night. He stops to sit with me and change his socks. I don't look at his feet, but I can smell enough to know that they're in bad shape. A few months ago, when it was still cold at night, Leah took Greg to the hospital for detox. He stayed long enough to wrestle with the shakes and sweats that rack a body when the demons are coming out. But he never took off his boots.

I love some of the old paintings of Jesus' ascension into heaven—the ones where the disciples look up in amazement and confusion as Jesus disappears into the clouds. Jesus' bare feet hang out of the clouds at the center of those pictures. Whatever their feelings, the disciples' eyes are on those feet, drawing my gaze to them as well, asking me to remember that Jesus has a body like mine and Greg's. Shaped from the dirt we walk on, our feet are made to touch the ground. On them we stand or run.

The Bible is not so lofty as to overlook instructions about what to do with our feet. "As shoes for your feet put on whatever will make you ready to proclaim the gospel of peace." I still have a pair of boots I bought when I was sixteen years old to wear as I rode a motorbike through the bush of Zimbabwe, showing the *Jesus* film in villages that didn't have electric lights. My feet were equipped for a life on the move, and the faith I inherited gave them plenty of reason to hit the road. But what does it take to be ready to speak peace in this place? What is the good news that Greg and I can celebrate together?

I asked that question of Darryl in the street that day, after he had told me about the records Greg set in the hundred-yard dash. "Nobody could have told me nothing when I was out there running," Darryl said. "I had to get tired before I learned to rest in the Lord." Maybe there is a grace in these bodies of ours, even in their wearing out and returning to the dust. We die to live again, stand still so we can learn to move on.

For a moment, while Greg changes his socks and I get ready to begin the day, we sit barefoot beside one another on the front porch, swapping stories. I say a prayer for grace to still us both and stretch this rest into eternity.

t the heart of the Benedictine tradition, stability is tied to a homemaking way of life. In the fourth chapter of his *Rule*, Benedict outlines a way of life for monks that had been passed down to him from multiple sources. Christian readers of these "tools for good works" can easily notice their source in the Ten Commandments, the Sermon on the Mount, and several of Paul's epistles. Scholars who have examined the list closely, comparing it with other ancient texts, say that it is a modification of a nonmonastic catalogue of instructions from the early church.

As challenging as the monastic way of life may seem, Benedict does not seem to think that it is essentially different from the life God invites all people to enjoy. Monasticism is the attempt to focus all of your energy on receiving the invitation to life in God's house. Though the particular vocation of the monk is not for everyone, its purpose is to point to a way of life that is good news for the whole world.

Benedict's conclusion to his list of tools is of particular interest to those of us who want to learn what the wisdom of stability offers for our daily life. "The workshop where we are to toil faithfully at all these tasks," he writes, "is the enclosure of the monastery and stability in the community." In Benedict's understanding of monastic life, all of the traditional practices of Christian faith—prayer, fasting, Scripture reading, works of mercy, hospitality, dying well, and the like—are given as tools to help us learn the "spiritual craft." Like woodworking or plumbing, the craft of life with God is learned by practicing it in apprenticeship to others who know the way better than ourselves. The tools we have inherited are of no more use to us by themselves than a trowel might be to someone who doesn't know a mason. But in a workshop we learn from others the craft of life with God, which is, like all crafts, embodied in a living tradition of practices. The name Benedict gives for this workshop is "stability in the community."

For Benedictines who share life together under the Rule, this image of the workshop is a constant reminder of the promises they made when they joined the particular community of their profession. Reflecting on the monastic promises, Peter the Venerable wrote, "If they keep the first vow [stability] they are held by the content of the second [the monastic way of life]. If they keep the second, they are bound by the constraints of the first." Monks who remain in the community where they make their vows learn the monastic rhythm from the brothers who welcome them into their common life. Likewise, part of inhabiting that living tradition of practices is choosing to stay and welcome others who come to learn the craft. In short, there is no stability without a way of life; no rhythm of life together without the commitment to stay.

If this is true for the monastery, it is also true to some extent for every community that seeks to learn the craft of life with God. Though the monastic vocation is peculiar to certain individuals and communities, the whole point of the church's setting people apart as monks is to reveal something of the good news Jesus offers all people. "Come unto me," Jesus beckons, calling all of us who are weary from wandering and heavy-laden by the burden of trying and trying again to make a home for ourselves. "Come unto me . . . and find rest for your souls; for my yoke is easy and my burden is light."

When Jesus invites us into the rest of his easy yoke, he is not saying that we can take it easy while he does all the work. Rest is not a couch where we kick back in front of the TV, glad to be home for the holidays. Rather, it is the place where we learn the rhythms of the work we were made for from the One who made us. Rest is coming home to the way of life that fits, learning to inhabit the story of God's people and practice the craft of life with God wherever we are.

If stability challenges us to stay put in a mobile world, its wisdom also promises a way of life that is sustainable, giving rest to weary souls. By sitting in their cells and looking the devil in the face, the desert mothers and fathers were able to name the powers that keep us from life with God. Seeing the problem clearly, they focused their attention on developing practices that made it possible to resist the devil's schemes.

This very practical pursuit of a life with God revealed to our desert forebears their utter dependence on the grace of God and other people. "One thing that comes out very clearly from any reading of the great desert monastic writers," says Anglican Archbishop Rowan Williams, "is the impossibility of thinking about contemplation or meditation or 'spiritual life' in abstraction from the actual business of living in the body of Christ, living in concrete community. The life of intimacy with God in contemplation is both the fruit and the course of a renewed style of living together." Again, we cannot rest in God without learning a new way of life with our neighbors. The craft of life with God is learned in the workshop of stability in community.

My own experience of staying put in Walltown has meant becoming an apprentice of a living tradition in community with other people. Trying to love my neighbors here means living in the face of ugly powers such as racism and addiction, poverty and abuse. These are not abstract social problems in our life together, but look much more like demons as they cripple friends, break relationships, and well up in my own soul, tempting me to violence or despair. More than once I have balled up my fist in a heated conversation, forgetting that our battle is not against flesh and blood. More often than I care to admit, I'm tempted to give up on others or myself. These demons are stronger than my will to do good.

But I have learned from the saints at our church to sing, "I will trust in the Lord 'til I die." The faith we affirm each

Sunday morning is more than a set of beliefs about who God is and what Jesus did for us on the cross two thousand years ago. It is that, for sure, but it is more. The faith we sing is a radical trust that the God who raised Jesus from the dead can save us now from the demons that have us by the neck. "I'm gonna stay on the battlefield," we shout, taunting the devil while we're together so we might remember Jesus' victory when we are facing the darkness alone. Faith is fuel for the struggle that we're engaged in here and now.

But it is still more. "I'm gonna treat everybody right," the song teaches us to say, celebrating the revolutionary love ethic of the One who died for us while we were yet sinners. Jesus is inviting us into a way of living that doesn't pass on the violence we receive, but rather absorbs it, returning good for evil. No, we don't live that way all the time. But we keep singing it. Staying in the workshop of this community gives me a place to learn what it might mean to sing this song with my whole life.

Apart from stability in the life of a community, the songs of Zion quickly begin to sound like wishful thinking. How dare we sing about the sweet by and by while our kids don't have health care and our teenagers are leaving the neighborhood in police cars and body bags? If our longing for home is just personal nostalgia, it is no better than the booze and dope that promise some short-term respite from the harsh reality around us. Fragile people in a broken neighborhood, we are susceptible to "crack religion" that sells Jesus as cheap comfort for whatever ails us.

But the practice of singing our faith comes alive in the workshop of stability. In the context of relationships that are held together by the grace of God, Mother McCrea and Deacon Buffaloe pass on the wisdom of faithful trust, constant struggle, and revolutionary love. I know our songs are not a pipe dream because I see how they have sustained saints in the hard fight of faith. As I apprentice myself to their wisdom, these songs are tools I am learning to use against the powers that tempt me to violence and despair. I am a slow learner, but I can feel the songs reaching deep inside of me. As they do their work, my clenched fists loosen and I reach out to others for the help that I need. Open and vulnerable to people who know me, I feel at home.

A School for Prayer

Brian, who teaches at a university in Scotland, told me the story about how his family decided where to live. When they moved to the university town that is now their home, they were immigrants from the United States, strangers to the local landscape and dependent on others for information about the place. A number of people in the university community suggested to them that the neighborhood around the school was less than desirable for a young family. Government-subsidized housing attracted under-resourced people. The crime rate was high and the schools were bad. Everyone offering advice suggested that their family would do best to buy a house outside of town, from which Brian could commute to work.

But Brian and his family were eager to make life work in one place. They had been frustrated when living in U.S. cities by the constant commute from home to work to school to church to shopping centers to playgrounds to home again. "Wouldn't it be great to do everything in one place?" they thought. So they got an apartment close to the university and started getting to know their neighbors.

After years of walking between his home, office, and church, Brian told me the best thing about stability in his community is that he can go to morning prayer at his local parish every day. Gathering with a small group of people to pray the Psalms each day establishes a rhythm for his life. Rooting his thoughts and prayers in the songs of God's people, this daily rhythm invites him to remember the full range of emotions we might experience in a life with God. Stability of place makes possible a workshop where he can learn to pray.

From the very beginning of the desert tradition, the Psalter was used as a school for instructing the soul in the language of life with God. Benedict devotes a full ten chapters of his Rule to instructions about how monks are to pray the psalms, exhorting the brothers not to complain about saying 150 psalms in a week since they know that the desert fathers, "energetic as they were, did all this in a single day." The monastic office for prayer has always been an ordered curriculum for those who would yoke themselves to the Psalter's wisdom.

The history of Christian liturgy reveals that this practice of gathering with other Christians to pray the Psalms has not been peculiar to monks and nuns. In addition to the monastic office, ancient church documents also record "cathedral offices"—outlines for common prayer that give an order for praying the Psalms morning and evening in local congregations. It was evidently not uncommon for ancient Christians to gather before work and again at the end of the day to say and sing psalms together, punctuating their lives with the rhythms of Israel's songs. Like Brian, most of them lived and worked within walking distance of the congregations they belonged to. Returning to that space and its prayers in a daily rhythm, scholars and laborers alike practiced the craft of life with God, students together in a school of prayer they had inherited.

The Psalms are a practical school for life with God, teaching language by immersion and inviting us into the lived reality of a community's story. From the very beginning, they hold up an image of stability as the goal toward which a good life is directed: "Happy are those who do not follow the advice of the wicked, or take the path that sinners tread, or sit in the seat of scoffers; but their delight is in the law of the LORD, and on his law they meditate day and night. They are like trees planted by streams of water, which yield their fruit in its season, and their leaves do not wither. In all they do, they prosper." The expressed aim of the psalmist is to put down roots that tap into streams of living water, and this longing for home directs the whole collection of songs, always bringing us back to our deepest longing.

Lest we romanticize the reality of life lived with particular people in a real place, however, the Psalms are also replete with realism about life in community. I never knew how many enemies I had until I started praying the Psalms every day. With raw emotion these songs give voice to the agony of broken relationships. "O LORD, how many are my foes!" we cry out together.

Some of our enemies are the kings of nations and corporations who make war and devour the poor. But most of them are closer to home. The Psalms understand the agony of betrayal because they are the songs of a broken people who have lived together. "It is not enemies who taunt me—I could bear that," we confess. What makes my stomach writhe is when I realize that I have been betrayed by "my equal, my companion, my familiar friend, with whom I kept pleasant company." This is, of course, when I am most tempted to think it's time to pack up my bags and leave. But the Psalms teach me the language of a people who stay, crying out to God and engaging the hard work of reconciliation with intimates who have become enemies.

Given this realism, the most surprising thing about the Psalms may be how often they turn to praise. Grounded in the messiness of real life and broken relationships, this language of adoration and exaltation is not tainted by the sentimentality that infects so much contemporary "praise music." The same psalm that begins with the question, "Will you forget me forever?" ends just five verses later with the declaration, "I will sing to the LORD, because he has dealt bountifully with me." Even God gets messy in this relationship, wrestling Israel all night long by the Jabbok River. But the struggle leads to clarity of language that stands out in contrast to the hesitancy of postmodern speech. "I will sing praises to my God all my life long," we say.

The sentiment is not just for the moment. Having found a sure foundation for our lives, we are able to commit. The God we learn to talk to in the Psalms is our God, binding us to a placed people. Singing their songs, we are invited to practice a craft that makes us into a community in the place where we are.

Finding Our Rhythm

A contemporary Benedictine sister from France, Lazare de Seilhac, observes how visitors to her monastery often admire the wisdom of the community's common schedule. Perhaps influenced by the need for spiritual retreat that brought them to the monastery in the first place, these visitors confess that they are frustrated by the difficulty of making space in their own daily lives for prayer and spiritual reading. So many demands and distractions seem to crowd out the prayer life that we know to be important but have a hard time justifying when the neighborhood association is meeting or the kids need breakfast or a conversation on the cell phone just seems easier. The monastic schedule inspires outsiders, Seilhac notes, helping us see that it is possible for a community to find its rhythm in a life with God.

But as someone who lives in submission to the monastic schedule, Seilhac also admits that the ordered life of a community can be frustrating, especially when a sister is just beginning the monastic life. "When the common timetable comes and interrupts a job which really requires a continuous length of time—then she is not always sure that the timetable contributes to profound peace of heart and soul." Maybe we don't need to live in monastic community to sympathize. Any parent who has struggled to get kids ready for church on Sunday morning can understand the tension between personal and family rhythms and the schedule of a larger community.

If personal peace of mind is the highest good we can imagine, life with other people becomes difficult, especially when we are divided by cultures, values, education, or class. This is, I suspect, why the church continues to be the most segregated institution in American society, even as schools, workplaces, and even families become racially integrated. A spirituality that seeks peace of mind leads almost inevitably to consumer religion that sells an experience on Sunday morning (or Saturday evening, if you prefer) to individuals who have little sense of community because they are rarely together in one place at the same time.

Given the expressed loneliness of so many individuals who have been displaced in the name of personal choice, Seilhac's reflection on the difficulty of entering into a monastic rhythm may have more to offer us outside the monastery than we suspect. "What does not seem on the scale of a single day to favor interior unity," she writes, "produces in time, with the passing of months and years, a sort of shift in the pole of confidence, a shift in one's inner dynamism. It is through the 'help from God' received through obedience and through holding fast to community life that one finds the capacity to complete one's tasks. It is the great rhythm of the prayer of the Office which becomes the rhythm of one's own person."

The divine office for Benedictines is the Opus Dei—the "work of God"—that is all of creation's true work. The trees of the fields clap their hands, deep calls out to deep, and even stones are poised to cry out in praise to the Creator. Likewise, the communion of saints around God's throne sings, "Holy, holy, holy," worshiping the Lamb who is worthy to receive all honor and glory. When Benedictines sing the Psalter and pray the prayers of the church on a fixed schedule, it is their privilege to devote their whole lives to the work for which every creature was made. The rhythm of their life together serves as an invitation to those of us outside the monastery: come and see how life with God reorders our relationship with time.

But this invitation comes at a time in human history when we are at odds with Father Time. For many of us in contemporary society, technology enables our desire to transcend the limitations of a twenty-four-hour day. We eschew any rhythm of life in hopes of doing everything at once. "Multitasking" is the current catchphrase for our attempt to be something more than creatures living within the limits of time. Our grandparents who moved from farms to factories in hope of a better life were pushed to beat the clock by bosses who checked their time cards and looked over their shoulders. But today, writes journalist Maggie Jackson, "we are our own efficiency experts, relentlessly driving ourselves to do more, ever faster." We pay a premium for the cell phones, computers, gadgets, and gizmos that promise us everything at once.

Interruption scientists have begun to study the effects of our obsession with multitasking on the work that we actually get done in a given day. After studying workers at two high-tech firms for more than one thousand hours, Gloria Mark reported that workers, on average, spend just eleven minutes on a project before switching to another. While focusing on a single project, they typically change tasks every three minutes. Perhaps this just demonstrates that we are, indeed, good at multitasking. But Mark's research also shows that, once distracted, workers take an average of twenty-five minutes to return to their interrupted task. For "knowledge workers" who put in an eight-hour day, more than a fourth of their work time is consumed by interruptions. Like a kid who jumps off the roof, convinced that he can defy gravity, we are beginning to feel the consequences of our disdain for the limits of time.

Could the stability of the monastery's rhythm be a gift to those of us who live outside its walls? For Saint Augustine, in the fifth century, the most fundamental distinction human beings need to understand is the difference between the Creator and creation. The condition of time is one way to understand this distinction. "Things which happen under the condition of time are in the future, not yet in being, or in the present, already existing, or in the past, no longer in being," Augustine wrote in his classic *City of God*. "But God comprehends all these in a stable and eternal present," Augustine noted, convinced that our fundamental stability depends on a God who is not like us and is, thereby, able to save us.

Such an understanding of God reveals that our desire to get out of the limits of time is, at root, a desire to become like God by our own efforts. This is what the Christian tradition calls sin. Sin consistently leads humans to self-destructive behavior, frustrating us not only because we don't get what we want but also because the things we want seem so noble and good. Who, after all, should we strive to be like, if not God? So long as we're doing good things, wouldn't it be better if we could do two or three or four of them at once? Maybe I could listen to Gregorian chant on my iPod while I jog to stay in shape. Someone else might get a daily e-mail with a prayer to say while they're balancing the budget for a nonprofit that feeds the hungry.

What we hardly ever want to admit is that we are limited creatures. Subject to the confines of time and space, we cannot be anywhere, anytime. As a matter of fact, we can only be in this place, now. Monastics who have accepted this as an ultimate reality and promised themselves to stability for life offer us a model for what it might look like to find our rhythm in a life of faith. Embracing the credo *ora et labora*—prayer and work—Benedictines have long practiced an ordered rhythm of gathering for prayer, scattering to take care of the day's tasks, and returning again to the call of the monastery's bell—sometimes as often as seven times a day. In this rhythm of daily life, time is transformed from an enemy into a friend. A nun said to me once, "Whatever else happens in a day, I know I get to come back to prayer soon enough." Anticipated like a good meal or a planned meeting with a friend, prayer is not an interrupting distraction but rather a gift that reminds us what all of our living is for.

Over time, we can see how the gift of a rhythm of life with God transforms a community and the world around it. The community of Sant'Egidio in Rome was started by high school students in 1968. Inspired by student protests, a handful of middle-class Roman youths got together and started talking about how to love their neighbors as themselves. They committed to pray together several times a week in the Church of Sant'Egidio. Forty years later, communities around the world continue to chant psalms and sing hymns each evening, rooting their members in a reality much older and deeper than their own desire to be friends.

Popular historian Thomas Cahill has written that Sant'-Egidio is "one of the very few great religious phenomena of our time," acknowledging that most people are tired of fraudulent religious phenomena—especially *Christian* religious movements. Sant'Egidio's movement stands out because their friendships have helped stabilize so many marginalized and forgotten people. An international movement with some sixty thousand members, Sant'Egidio runs HIV/AIDS clinics in Africa, feeds thousands of homeless people in Rome, and has started homes for abandoned elderly and mentally handicapped people around the world. When the United Nations wrote its report on the peace agreement that ended Mozambique's civil war, they attributed Sant'Egidio with arranging the settlement between the guerillas and the government.

If stability is indeed a craft we learn as we settle into the good work of making a life with God, we would do well to join the community of Sant'Egidio as apprentices to the rhythms of prayer that precede us. Some of these are written in prayer books, while others are best learned by sitting close to someone in worship, letting the stomp of their feet and the clap of their hands reverberate through your body. Wherever we find them, though, these rhythms are our link to the eternal dance of the seraphim around the throne of God. In them we learn the cadence of life that lasts forever, interrupting this world's broken systems even now with signs of hope.

Visiting

allace is skilled in the art of visiting, having learned it firsthand from a master—his mother, Ms. Carolyn. If I catch them both on the porch at the same time, I might as well cancel my plans, whatever they were. I'm going to be here a while.

Most any story is fair game for front porch visits, so long as you tell it well. It doesn't have to be new. Indeed, some of the best stories get told over and over again. Last week at church we buried Mr. Wall, the oldest living descendent of the Wall family, for whom Walltown is named. Mr. Wall was a walker, even into his nineties, so everyone has a story to tell about offering Mr. Wall a ride (he often refused them) or seeing him push a lawn mower clear across town. Mr. Wall was also a storyteller. To remember him is to tell the stories he used to tell about this place and its people. Half an hour later, we're still sitting around telling stories.

This way of life is fragile, and folks around here know it. Our Mr. Walls are dying, and times are changing in Walltown. The conversation turns to issues in the neighborhood, and someone mentions the widely held suspicion that people with money might eventually push us out. This gives Ms. Carolyn the opportunity to recite one of her favorite monologues—the one about how-I'm-gonna-sell-out-to-the-highest-bidder-and-buy-a-motor-home, which she has perfected, almost like a good sermon. I love how at the end, when her eyes are wide and she's yelling a little, Ms. Carolyn will say, "Don't ya'll worry. I ain't leaving for good. I'll still roll through here and wave at ya'll every once in a while."

What, after all, would be the point of seeing the world in a Winnebago if you didn't come back to tell the story? And what is the point of a community—of a life, even—if we don't sit down and take the time to enjoy it by remembering?

One block down, at the bottom of the hill, I walk past Ms. Annie's house on the opposite side of the street. Since she fell and broke her hip a few months ago, Ms. Annie has been in the nursing home. After I visited her there a few weeks ago, her daughter told me she was afraid Ms. Annie would never come home again. But as I look both ways to cross Englewood Avenue, I notice Ms. Annie, at home in her wheelchair, sitting on her front porch. She is talking to a neighbor— "visiting," we say around here—hanging on to the life she knows for whatever time remains.

4
ROOTS OF LOVE

When it comes to the practice of stability, I have a mixed heritage. My mother, the eldest daughter of a mendicant musician, moved twenty-eight times before she started high school. With three daughters to raise in early midlife, my maternal grandfather settled down in King, North Carolina. Driving a Greyhound bus during the week and touring with the family band on the weekend kept him going. But Mom was glad to stay put. She fell in love with a local boy and married him right out of high school. Excepting an act of God, she'll never move again.

Mom's need for stability fit well with my dad's story. As far back as anyone can remember, his people have lived in Stokes County, North Carolina. Our English name suggests a family tree rooted across the Atlantic Ocean, but all of our memories are grounded in the red dirt at the base of Saura-town Mountain. My dad grew up out of that soil, priming tobacco and paying attention to the local scene. As a kid I was often amazed that he knew the names of every plant that grew in the yards of folks we would visit on Sunday afternoons. He knew them like he knew the second cousins of our hosts, and Dad asked about both with the same genuine interest. He never got bored. Every detail of the place mattered to him.

Once when Mom and Dad were dating, driving with the windows down, they passed a tobacco field that had just been plowed. Dad smiled. "Sure is beautiful, ain't it?"

Nervous with new love on a bright spring day, Mom was quick to celebrate beauty, but a bit hesitant to admit her confusion about just what Dad was admiring. "Sure is," she said. "And, uh, what part is most beautiful to you?"

"I mean the way the dirt looks, turned over like that in the sun."

At sixteen, Mom didn't yet appreciate the beauty of dirt, nor did she understand, exactly, why it mattered. But after more than thirty years in the place, having raised her own boys there (washing more of that red clay out of our clothes than she cares to remember, I'm sure), Mom remembered Dad's comment one spring day and told it to me with a smile. Grafted onto the local scene, she too has become a lover of the place—even of its dirt. Like the minerals that rise through roots to grow a tree planted in the ground, the land has gotten inside of her, claiming its place in her heart.

To practice stability is to learn to love both a place and its people. The twelfth-century Benedictine Anselm of Canterbury compared a restless monk to a tree that, after being "frequently transplanted or often disturbed," will not take root anywhere, but only withers and dies. "If he often moves from place to place at his own whim, or remaining in one place is frequently agitated by hatred of it," Anselm observes, then the unhappy monk "never achieves stability with roots of love."

Anselm's warning is stern, but I love the idea that the stability we are made for helps us establish "roots of love," binding us intimately to our landscape and the people who share life on it. How else can we learn the attention that is needed to really know a community? How else would we ever gain the patience that is required to care for a place over time?

Without roots of love, we easily become slaves to our own desires, using the place where we happen to be as a staging ground for our ambitions and manipulating the people around us so they might serve our objectives. We do this, of course, with the best of intentions—even in God's name. But until we give ourselves to a place—until we care enough to learn the names of its flowers and its second cousins—stability's wisdom suggests we cannot know very much about the One who so loved the world that he gave his only begotten Son.

Stability teaches us something about the importance of particularity. God's omnipotence and omnipresence may be attributes we can contemplate in the abstract realm of ideas, but the love of God is as particular as a Jewish man named Jesus who was born of a woman named Mary in a town called Bethlehem. We know what love looks like when we know it among particular people in a given place. If the love of God and neighbor is our end goal, roots of love in stability are the means God has given for making progress in this life.

The practice of stability, then, is an exercise in putting down roots. A good tree bears good fruit, we know, and the fruit of the Spirit begins with love. But we are product-oriented people, eager to skip over the process and enjoy the apple without attending to the soil and sun and roots that help it grow. All of us would love to be more loving, but we spend precious little time establishing roots of love. Without them, though, the tree withers and there is neither fruit nor shade nor a branch to tie a swing on and enjoy a summer evening. If I really want to learn to love my neighbor, I have to pay attention to the details of life in this place. Stability's wisdom calls me to learn the ways and means of grafting onto this place.

The Drip Line

Look at a tree on the landscape out your window and you will notice that it is shaped something like a geyser, reaching up in the single column of a trunk to spray out in limbs, most of them bending back toward the ground. Follow the downward slope of those bending branches as if they were the fluid spray of the geyser, and you can sketch out a circumference on the ground around the trunk of any tree. That circle is called the "drip line." Without digging below the surface, it offers a pretty good sketch of how far away from a tree its roots reach for the water and nutrients it needs to flourish.

Trees vary a great deal in size, and any tree, given the time, can extend its reach through growth. But it is important for the life of a tree that its extension above the surface not exceed its growth below. Stability depends on a tree knowing that its root system beneath the surface limits its capacity to send out limbs and produce fruit. In short, everything depends on the drip line.

For people on the go, the root system that a drip line traces may feel more like a limit than a gift. Tight-knit community can feel suffocating, as a Korean friend who grew up in an immigrant neighborhood reminds me. When I listen closely to my neighbors, I hear the same concern. When you've never had a chance to get away from the confines of a place that can feel stifling, it's hard to celebrate limits to personal freedom.

Yet, the Psalms invite us to name limits that are life-giving, sketching for us the drip lines of our lives. "The boundary lines have fallen for me in pleasant places," we pray. "I have a goodly heritage." Such an embrace of what is given surprises our modern spirits, sometimes even raising concerns that such an attitude might encourage resignation to the status quo. Surely we cannot simply accept self-satisfied provincialism or imposed limitations based on a history of injustice. Yes, we inherit some good in every tradition and culture. But our heritage is always a mixed bag, also passing on to us boundaries that mark histories of division. Walk south from my house and you'll notice when you cross Green Street that the houses are bigger, the lawns are manicured, and the kids playing badminton in the yard are white. Boundary lines, we know, tell a story, and we are people well trained in the critical skills of deconstruction.

But for all our legitimate resistance to boundaries, stability invites us to learn how the limits of a root system can be life-giving. Paul Wilkes, who has written about his experience of learning from monastic wisdom, reflects on his resistance to limits as a young person, saying, "I bridled at restraints; I moved again and again. There was always something more out there I wasn't finding." For Wilkes, this led to a midlife crisis about the true meaning of freedom. "I looked upon married life and children as punishingly restrictive and certainly not a path to holiness or heroism," he confesses. "After my devoted attempt to be a man of the world, I swerved onto other paths, believing I needed to live with the poor, then to be a monk, do some work of great value to humankind. Something out of the ordinary." All of this frenetic searching eventually led Wilkes to what he calls a "desperately unhappy existence." Free to pursue any life he could imagine, Wilkes found himself unable to really live.

Considering the practice of stability some two decades after this crisis, Wilkes is able to name how his own salvation has depended on accepting the limits of marriage. "With two sons embarking on their teenage years and a working wife, my freedom of movement is severely restricted, my own desires secondary at best. Yet I experience some of the richest days of my life." No longer free to do whatever he wants, Wilkes sees that he *is* free to love particular people whose needs he knows. To be sure, that circle of people is limited, circumscribed by the drip line of his life. But as he establishes roots of love, Wilkes can see that he is now able to grow. The boundary lines of his life and love expand as his roots grow deeper.

Stability's dependence on boundary lines helps us to understand an aspect of monastic life that is often confusing to outsiders—namely, the practice of "enclosure," whereby monastics separate themselves from the world around them and its influences. I remember visiting a monastery as a teenager and being put off by a sign that informed me I was not welcome in the monastic gardens. I had just heard one of the brothers give a talk on hospitality. "Some kind of welcome that is," I thought to myself.

But the monastic tradition knows that we cannot become the gift to others we are called to be until we embrace the limits that are necessary to our vocation. "There is a need for some structures to preserve the distinctiveness that flows from generations of monastic living," writes contemporary Benedictine and spiritual writer Michael Casey. "Whatever the idiocies associated with the interpretation of canonical enclosure in the past, it needs to be recognized that too many foreign invasions undermine the monastic seriousness of the community." Acknowledging the dangers of boundaries, monastics also know that they are necessary if we are to grow into the fullness of what God has made us to be.

Growing up in the place that my mom and dad love so well, I was as put off by its limits as I was by that sign I read outside the monastic gardens. Not only bored by the ordinariness of my hometown, I was also angry at its prejudices, convinced that the racism I witnessed on our church steps was a consequence of folks not broadening their minds through interaction with other people and places. (I was a reader; I knew everyone didn't think the way we did.) I wanted to break free from the confines of rural life and do something great for God. That meant moving somewhere else.

Living outside the South, I learned that people in other places have their prejudices too. It didn't take long to see that folks who talked like me were looked down on as uneducated or laughed at as naive (notice, sometime, which characters in cartoons have the Southern accents). Mimicking the trusted voices of the nightly news, I learned to speak as if I were from no place at all. But after forsaking my people and place, I didn't know who I was or which "issues" really mattered. I knew enough to know that I still needed to grow up, but without a drip line to sketch out the root system of my life, I wasn't sure where to start.

Growing into our promise of stability here in Walltown, I've begun to see how much my own vocation depends on embracing the boundary lines of my people in North Carolina. Yes, we have our prejudices and our demons—a history whose ghosts still haunt us. But so does everyone else. This story is my story, its complexities ones that I know. Its textures are in the dirt my people have farmed and in the stories we tell one another—even in the drawl we use to tell them. I know our story well enough that I can weigh it against the story of God's people, noting the tensions and praying for grace to be born again and again in God's family. I'm not sure what I might be called to somewhere else, but here in this place I know my vocation is to interrupt the racial segregation of Christian churches, to celebrate beloved community as an answer to our loneliness, and to make Jesus my Lord rather than my copilot.

What sort of fruit do we bear by accepting where our boundary lines have fallen and giving thanks for a goodly heritage? Truth is, we cannot know ahead of time. "We plant seeds that one day will grow. We water seeds already planted, knowing that they hold future promise," wrote Archbishop Oscar Romero after he had embraced the struggle of his Salvadoran people by questioning the injustice at the heart of a system he served. "We may never see the end results, but that is the difference between the master builder and the worker." It is also the difference between the tree and the One who created it with the potential to grow and bear fruit. What we can do is the hard work of knowing and loving the people and place within our drip line. What will come of it, we say in hope, is in God's hands.

Tapping into a Support System

To embrace the limits of a place is to learn to look at the people around us with fresh expectation. "These are the people God has given for the sake of my salvation," we can say as we look at our family, neighbors, coworkers, or fellow church members. Whether these people are easy to love is not the question. Stability invites us to ask, "How are they gifts from God to help me grow in love?"

Augustine Roberts, a contemporary Benedictine, writes about how his community loves their order for the love of God. But Roberts goes further to note that "love of the Order is made concrete in love of the community and its members, of *these* members, of this brother at my side. Stability depends on this. Without this living bond of love, stronger than any other tie, stability of spirit is impossible and bodily stability is devoid of value."

The practice of stability cannot be sustained without the "living bond of love" that is established when we give ourselves to people as they are. As helpful as the image of a tree may be, the root system we are invited to tap into may be better imagined as a rhizome weed, holding fast not so much because of any one shoot's strength, but by virtue of the whole root system's being tied together beneath the surface. Like crabgrass, our stability depends on that connection with every other blade of grass—most immediately with "this brother at my side," as Roberts notes. The whole system depends on my recognizing the person next to me as a gift.

No doubt, each of us longs for this connection with other people. We have invested much of our best time and talent in developing and mastering technologies of connection. Beginning with the telegraph a little over a century ago, we learned that it was possible for two people in different places to communicate with one another. From the telephone to the cell phone, we have mastered this technology of person-to-person contact.

But we are hyperconnectional people. Not satisfied to overcome the limits of space with one person at a time, we imagined social networks that make it possible for us to be in touch with any number of our friends in any number of places *at the same time*. As of the end of 2009, the Internet social networking site Facebook had 350 million users worldwide—all people who are tied into a network of friends, communicating with one another around the clock. The rhizome has grown to cover the whole earth, it seems, giving us the potential to reach out and touch virtually everyone.

But there is nothing in our technology that helps us see the person next to us as a gift. Technologies that might facilitate friendship easily distract us from the joys and responsibilities of shared life with the people in front of us. A friend told me about a recent visit with her son during his freshman year of college. Eager to catch up, she took him out to dinner at a local restaurant. Looking up from her food during the meal, she noticed his head hanging down across from her. "Is something wrong?" she asked. "No, Mom. I'm just sending a quick text under the table," her son replied.

"Daydreaming" was once the temptation of romantics who knew their imaginations could disengage from the local scene and contemplate what life might be like somewhere else. Today it threatens to become a way of life for a society whose technology so easily wags it by the tail. The great advantage of a Facebook friendship, of course, is that it is so easy. I get to choose who I want to "friend" and whose friendship requests I respond to. We gather around our common interests, share the stuff we want others to know, and log off when we feel like it. In many ways what we have is connection without obligation. But intimacy without commitment is what our society has traditionally called "infidelity."

As with adultery in marriage, the problem of infidelity isn't so much that it breaks a rule as it is that it destroys the fabric of trust that sustains a healthy community. (In a troubled marriage, no one feels this more intensely than the kids.) If our relationships with other people do not entail responsibility and obligation, they are easily reduced to self-serving transactions in a marketplace where everyone else is always trying to sell us something—or worse, to sell us themselves. Such a commodification of life denies in practice the fundamental claim of God's economy—that all is gift and life is a mystery of divine love.

Speaking to his Cistercian brothers, Roberts writes, "Your monastery and community are for you a *grace*, a gift from God, and a *mission*, a task to accomplish. We are responsible for the growth of those with whom we live and for the salvation of many persons. The harmonious development of the entire Church depends on our stability in this community." Benedictines live within a tradition that helps them name their responsibility to one another and the world as both gift and task. Whether we share the living tradition of an order, though, all of us have reason to be concerned about the harmonious development of the world around us. If human life depends on people establishing roots of love in particular communities where we graft onto networks that sustain life, then stability is never embraced more fully than in a faithful relationship with my neighbor.

Learning to Bend

One of the wise mothers of the Egyptian desert, Amma Theodora, told this story about a monk who became frustrated with his neighbor and wanted to move.

> There was a monk, who, because of the great number of his temptations said, "I will go away from here." As he was putting on his sandals, he saw another man who was also putting on his sandals and this other monk said to him, "Is it on my account that you are going away? Because I go before you wherever you are going."

Like the monk in Theodora's story, most of us prefer to avoid confrontation with our neighbors. If someone is an enemy, we usually have language to say why "we" cannot get along with "them." Like a sword, we use such language to defend against the attacks of a named adversary. With people closer to us, though, we often don't know how to say just why they bother us. Our tensions with neighbors are more complex for a whole host of reasons, not the least of which is that we don't have the words to say why they get under our skin. Usually it is easier to just say to ourselves, "I will go away from here." Maybe, we reason, the problem is a personality conflict. There's no need to make a scene. We'll just move on.

But the brash honesty of the desert tradition will not let us get away with such a vague justification for separating ourselves from the root system on which our stability depends. As if from nowhere, the neighbor we didn't want to confront shows up to ask, "Is it on my account that you are going away?" Not waiting for the lie we would be tempted to say in response, our neighbor drops the full weight of reality in front of us with a single sentence: "I go before you wherever you are going."

If we are honest about life in human community, we must admit that the people closest to us are not only our connection points in a support system that we depend on for our very lives. They are that, for sure, but they are also mirrors who reflect the hidden shadows of our souls. The monk in Theodora's story is right: we do face temptations when we open ourselves to relationship with neighbors. But if we think we can flee from those temptations by getting away from the neighbor, we deceive ourselves. The neighbor goes before us wherever we go, forcing us to confront the wound we carry with us.

Jean Vanier was an accomplished man in early adulthood. The son of an influential family in Canada, he traveled the world, served as an officer in the Royal Navy, and completed a PhD in philosophy. By any outward measure of success, he was doing very well. But Vanier felt like something wasn't right. He went to a priest for counsel and asked him what he should do with his life. The priest told him to move in with a few disabled men who had recently been released from an institution. For Vanier, this was the beginning of a difficult conversion. He was unable to make life together work with one of the men. Life with the two that remained, Raphael and Philippe, was not easy. But in the struggle, Vanier learned something important from them. "The cry of people with disabilities was a very simple cry: do you love me? That's what they were asking," Vanier writes. "And that awoke something deep within me because that was also my fundamental cry."

Living close to people who could not deny their own brokenness, Vanier learned to name his own basic need for love. The healing he experienced became good news to others, many of whom wanted to come and learn with him from people with disabilities. This led to a community called L'Arche—French for "the ark"—which now has more than 120 sites around the world. Why have thousands of people been drawn to live as neighbors to people who have a disability—those whom L'Arche communities name "core members"? Maybe it is because, like Vanier, most of us need the help of a neighbor who will reveal to us our fundamental cry for love and the need to find it in a root system that ties us to other people.

Lisa told me that is why she joined a L'Arche community. I asked her if she had experienced the healing that Vanier describes in relationship with people who have disabilities. "Yes," she told me, "I've loved living with the core members. But I'm not sure whether I can stay," she confessed. "It's so hard to live with the other assistants." Less able to admit their own weakness and vulnerability, the able-bodied members of Lisa's community were the most difficult to deal with. Like her in so many ways, they constantly reflected back to her the things she least liked about herself.

Just as stability depends on our acknowledging our limits and our need for other people, it also demands of us a willingness to engage the neighbor who most annoys us. Establishing roots of love means coming to terms with the boundaries of our drip line and plugging into the root system that extends beneath the surface, giving life to an organic community of mutual dependence. But it also means bumping up against other people and weathering the storms that will inevitably come. The shape of every tree, both above and below the ground, is determined by the conditions in which it grows. When a root runs into solid rock, it finds a way to grow around it. Buffeted by storms, a tree that is firmly established knows how to give a little, bending so as not to break under pressure.

In human community, growth in love does not just happen. Even if we stay in a place, our impulse is to build walls to protect ourselves from the pain of seeing our own neediness in someone else's brokenness. A stubborn commitment to stay will not save us by itself. But Jesus, who said, "Abide in me as I abide in you," also gives the community that gathers in his name a way to confront the inevitable tensions in our relationships and engage the process of reconciliation. A stable life within the root system of real community depends upon this practice of forgiveness.

The occasion for Jesus' teaching on the practice of forgiveness in Matthew's Gospel is a fight among the disciples about which of them is the greatest. Lest we idealize the apostles, all of the Gospel writers make it clear that their fellowship was every bit as ego-charged and conflicted as ours are. In the midst of their life together, the disciples come to Jesus with a question that reveals their ambitious struggle: "Who is the greatest in the kingdom of heaven?" Jesus answers with a call to conversion: "Unless you change and become like children, you will never enter the kingdom of heaven."

Living in real relationship with our neighbors, we will inevitably butt heads. If we live close enough that we see through our masks and know one another as we are, my ambitions will at some point conflict with yours. Imagining the world as a pyramid upon which only one person can sit at the top, we strive to be great by becoming better than the person next to us. Despite the best of intentions, this fundamental wound at the center of ourselves leads us to hurt one another. Jesus knows this. His entire purpose in taking on human flesh was to save us from this condition by forgiving what we cannot fix. In doing so, Jesus invites us into the practice of forgiveness that sustains life together, making roots of love possible.

"If any member of the church sins against you," Jesus says, "go and point out the fault when the two of you are alone." Conflict will come in community, Jesus says. It does us no good to ignore it or to pretend that it will go away if we just move on to some new place. If someone wrongs me in pursuit of their own ambitions, I am instructed to pull them aside and talk about it. "If the member listens to you, you have regained that one," Jesus says. The purpose of the confrontation is not to vent my anger or to "get something off my chest." It is to regain a friend that I have lost. The point is reconciliation.

But Jesus knows that in our brokenness we often fail to see our need for one another. In the practice of forgiveness, then, we are called to rely on help from the community. "But if you are not listened to, take one or two others along with you. . . . If the member refuses to listen to them, tell it to the church." Inviting others into our conflicts is not easy. When angry, we are tempted to complain to friends who will sympathize with us, reinforcing our idea of the offender as an enemy. But one or two others who know and love both of us—or the whole community in which we share life together with our offender—force us to be honest about what's really going on. We cannot hide from our own need to be changed.

What happens, though, if someone refuses to change, even when confronted in love by the entire community? "If the offender refuses to listen even to the church," Jesus says, "let such a one be to you as a Gentile and a tax collector." In the Jewish community that Jesus inhabited, Gentiles and tax collectors were commonly recognized as outsiders and sellouts. They were the people who lived outside the drip line of the community's common life. Seeing the boundary as an enemy line, many people felt justified in their hatred of these outsiders, cursing them and keeping themselves pure by refusing to associate with "sinners and tax collectors."

Jesus, however, taught a love of enemies that was based on the strong conviction that the door to God's house always stands open. Without ignoring the need for boundaries that label some as insiders and some as outsiders, Jesus redefined what it looks like to live as a child of God. If Jesus is our example, then treating someone like a Gentile and a tax collector means forgiving them with extra grace, showering on them the kind of unconditional love that might convince them to come home and embrace the family on whom they've turned their backs. Lest anyone be confused about the process, thinking that after we've finished all the steps, we can give up on someone, Jesus replies to Peter's bold claim that he might be willing to go through the process as many as seven times to win someone back into the fellowship, "I tell you, not seven times, but seventy times seven." We might as well stop counting.

Church Communities International is a movement of people who know well the limits and struggles of a life dedicated to love of neighbor. They began living together under Germany's Nazi regime in the 1930s. Persecuted for their commitment to gospel pacifism, the community fled to Austria, where they were again run out by the Nazis. They settled in England for a short time, but were suspect during the war because they were Germans. Fleeing to South America, they struggled to survive the tropical climate. Finally, they planted themselves in New York and Pennsylvania in the 1950s. With communities today in the United States, England, Germany, and Australia, the movement stands out as a radical witness to the way of Jesus lived out by families and single people of all ages.

I asked Pete, a fellow who grew up in their New York community and has studied the movement's history, if he could tell me what practices he thought contributed to the stability of their communities through so many trials over the past eighty years. I was surprised by the simplicity of his answer. "We have the rule of Christ—Matthew 18." Giving themselves to the practice of forgiveness according to Jesus' teaching in Matthew 18, they have established roots of love, even in rocky soil.

A Place for Fighting

I am driving home with my windows down on a summer afternoon, hoping the wind will cool my head and maybe even blow the to-do list in the console out of reach. A neighbor sits on his porch, rocking in the shade. "All right," I holler with my hand out the window, slowing down for a brief exchange.

"I'm mad at you," he says.

He's asking for an argument, about what I do not know. If I get into it now I'll never get started on the supper that's due on our table in ninety minutes. I have promises to keep. But I make a note to get back to my neighbor—grab the to-do list and add one more thing for later. It's worth the time to walk down and follow up when I'm not in a hurry. Among their other good uses, front porches are for fighting.

I remember when my son, JaiMichael, was little—still riding on my shoulders—we sat on that same porch and witnessed a feud between two neighbors. It was his introduction to this tradition of fighting in public to make sure both sides fight fair. Voices got loud as both parties wove humor with criticism in a tapestry half crafted to win the argument, half performed to entertain the crowd. I wondered if it was too much for JaiMichael, so I swung him down into my lap. His eyes wide, he was busy processing. I decided to stay.

Even under the best of conditions, people cannot live together without conflict. Given our history of betrayal and abuse, infidelity and neglect, it's a wonder that folks here don't strangle one another with their bare hands. The occasional violence that rips the delicate fabric of Walltown is a reminder of how dangerous fights can be. But for the most part, folks around here keep it to words said on the porch. Having given it a place and made it an art, they've turned conflict into a community-building activity.

Supper is over now, JaiMichael is in bed, and I look out the window, watching dusk settle on this place. "Don't let the sun go down on your anger," the Scriptures say, reminding me that I've bumped into people today, like every day. I've not grown out of conflict. But I can learn to face the broken relationships that fragment my life. I can learn to fight—and fight fair. This, too, is growth.

I recall a poem from the place where I was born, recorded by the woman who taught me to tend to the written word. I learned the words in junior high school. Though I left my home, the words have not left me. Grafting them onto another place, I begin to see their meaning.

The house was built in '98,

prior to my arrival.

And a big maple tree at the corner of the

porch

was run over and buried lots of times by

wagons

moving in materials to build the house.

And the other maples what Daddy had

planted,

they had no trouble at all.

But they all died and this one lived that

had such rough treatment.

And there's a saying

"Rough weather makes good timber."

It may be

that the trouble with folks today

is that they're raised like hothouse

flowers,

and they don't have much to go on

at the end.

hen Abba Antony went out into the Egyptian desert to practice a life of prayer, he saw that the challenge was to stand his ground against the devil, trusting God for provision and committing not to flee when attacked. The desert monastics conceived of stability as a cosmic struggle. Echoing the combat imagery of Scripture, they aimed to "be strong in the Lord and in the strength of his power," taking up the weapons of prayer and fasting so that they might "stand against the wiles of the devil." When Christians in the cities heard reports about the exploits of these spiritual athletes, their communities were abuzz with tales of ascetic adventure in the wilderness. Stability never sounded so exhilarating.

As it turned out, though, stories about wrestling demons and fighting temptations were much more exciting to tell among friends in the city than they were to live in real time, alone in an arid place. Charged with adrenaline and a clear sense of who the enemy was, many a soul set out to fight only to find that somewhere along the way the whole effort lost its focus, and boredom set in. "Tell me again," they said to God or to themselves (for there was no one else to ask), "what am I doing here?"

John Cassian was a young man who heard the early monastic stories and made the rounds to sit at the feet of some of the desert's most acclaimed teachers. The abbas told him the truth about stability's challenges, describing the "noonday devil" who attacks *after* one commits to stay and begins to feel the heat of high noon. Writing about what he heard, Cassian described acedia—literally, a lack of care—as a spiritual malady that is "akin to sadness and is the peculiar lot of solitaries and a particularly dangerous and frequent foe of those dwelling in the desert." Reporting on the early monastic struggles with stability, Cassian named the midday demons we all have to face if we're going to stay put.

When the joy of morning wore off in the desert, the hard part about staying was that it got boring. And hot. With the sense of adventure gone, Cassian reported, new temptations set in, making the monk "horrified at where he is, disgusted with his cell, and also disdainful and contemptuous of the brothers who live with him or at a slight distance, as being careless and unspiritual." Unhappy in the place where they were, desert monastics were tempted to give up, to think they were not up to the task, or to wonder if they might not be of better service to God elsewhere. Once acedia set in, putting down roots of love seemed impossible.

In a hypermobile culture where we are always on the go, we who hear the call to stay might imagine ourselves as a type of spiritual athlete, not unlike the desert monastics who aimed to do combat on the cosmic frontlines. If our analysis has any truth to it, staying is indeed a defiant act of resistance against the spirit of the age. But standing against the seas of constant change also means acknowledging that stability is a practice fraught with contradictions and tensions, making us susceptible to temptations we would not otherwise have occasion to know.

The good news is that the tradition also offers tactics for subverting the schemes of these midday demons that will inevitably assail us. Naming them is here, as always, a first step toward resisting the devil's schemes. When Antony faced acedia, we are told, he cried out, "Lord, I want to be saved but these thoughts do not leave me alone. What shall I do in my affliction? How can I be saved?" Outside his cell, Antony saw a monk making rope, getting up to pray, sitting down to work again, then getting up again to pray. When he heard the Lord speak to him, Antony understood that he had been watching an angel, sent in answer to his prayer. "Do this and you will be saved," the angel said to Antony.

Crafty though they may be, the demons that come to attack us midway along our journey are not stronger than the rock in whom we trust. They are, however, stronger than we are. "How can I be saved?" Antony cries out, confessing both weakness and ignorance about how God might rescue him. His cry for help is a prayer to the One who has unmasked the demons and exposed their illusory power. Though he can do nothing to help himself, Antony at least knows on whom to call.

But God does not, seemingly, respond. Antony's biographer, Athanasius, records a memorable story about how, when the holy man was attacked by a vicious demon in his cell, Antony called on the name of Jesus and his attacker vanished. The story is compelling, but also strikingly different from this story about Antony's midday struggle. Here God does not intervene to aid Antony in the fight. Instead, a very down-to-earth angel offers an example. Some battles, it seems, are ours to fight.

But God does offer an example—a rhythm of prayer and manual labor that, over time, can help us shake the stranglehold of spiritual boredom. Where we might want a quick fix, God gives us work to do. Our struggle against the midday demons reminds us that staying is itself a process, as growth is the product of struggle. Salvation may not come like a SWAT team to rescue us in our time of crisis, but it does come. We are made new as we work out the salvation we're given "with fear and trembling."

The practice of stability cannot be reduced to a quick fix for the spiritual anxiety of a placeless people. It is a process. It takes time. Like college students who pop caffeine pills to stay up late, then drink double shots of espresso to make it through morning classes, we are prone to reach for an antidote that addresses our immediate needs. But stability will not work like a drug. If our feelings of rootlessness are what drive us to the practice, we'll need something more than an immediate sense of relief to help us stay. "Joy comes in the morning," the psalmist says (30:5), and there is, likewise, a honeymoon period after we've struggled through the decision to stay and commit to a place and people. But the demons we must overcome in order to commit are not the same as those we struggle against as we stay. To persevere in the process that leads to real growth, we must learn to name and resist the midday demons.

Ambition's Whisper

Gordon Cosby moved to Washington, DC, in the late 1940s to start Church of the Savior, a church based on small groups long before small groups became a strategy for church growth among nondenominational evangelicals. Committed to radical discipleship and social engagement—what Cosby called the "inward journey and the outward journey"—Church of the Savior became well known for holistic mission while most American Christians were still divided between a commitment to the "social gospel" and an emphasis on personal salvation. By the 1960s, word had gotten out about this interesting experiment in Christian discipleship. Cosby was flooded with invitations to travel and speak about Church of the Savior. Like Abba Antony before him, Cosby was called from his cell by seekers and friends alike.

Seeing these speaking engagements as an opportunity to extend Church of the Savior's ministry, Cosby initially accepted as many as he could. Increasingly, though, he was unsure how to balance the local work of pastoring a church with this national speaking ministry. In the midst of his confusion, Cosby heard God speak to him in an undeniable way. The message was simple: "Stay home and do your knitting."

Reflecting on his ministry nearly half a century later, Cosby looks back on that vocational struggle as a turning point in his life and in the life of Church of the Savior. He decided to turn down the speaking invitations and focus on the people God had gathered in a small community. His "knitting," as it turned out, was not very exciting work most days. It included a lot of listening to people, trying to hear what God was up to in their lives. It looked like prayer, especially with people who were confused or felt like they had failed. It meant paying attention to people's gifts and encouraging them. For over half a century, Cosby spent his best energies finding ways to support the things people felt called to when they listened to God's heart.

By any assessment, the Church of the Savior's ministry over the past fifty years has had an influence disproportionate to the relatively small size of its membership. In 2008 alone, 800 people found jobs and 325 new housing units were built through its ministries in Washington, DC. The founder of Fellowship of Christian Athletes (FCA) and a moderator of the Reformed Church in America have been raised up from among this flock. Progressive evangelical leader Jim Wallis wrote in 1997 that Church of the Savior "has had more influence around the country than any other church I know about." Like the trees in the book of Revelation that bear fruit in every season, this community of faith has grown into the abundance of divine fertility.

Of course, no one can say for sure what Gordon Cosby's influence might have been had he not listened to the gentle voice that invited him to stay home and do his knitting. But the young man from Church of the Savior who told me the story about Cosby's decision to stay put believes it has made all the difference for their community. Without Cosby's commitment to tend the orchard, he says, there would be no fruit.

Many of us who choose stability will have to struggle, as Cosby did, with the midday demon of ambition. Its voice is subtle, often suggesting new and exciting things that are undeniably good work. Ambition's suggestions are deceptively attractive because they can rarely be dismissed outright. There is, after all, no way to say beforehand what sort of extended vocation healthy growth might lead to. God's people in any place may be called to put out new branches, consider new ministries, even extend our boundaries beyond the limits we had initially imagined. To refuse growth outright is to contradict nature, like the feet that were once bound by Chinese emperors for the sake of an ideal of beauty that debilitated the women it was forced upon. Some growth is natural for any living creature.

But ambition tempts us to forsake the mundane for the sake of unlimited growth—or, at least, new opportunities. We are so easily unimpressed by the ordinary, longing for the feeling of excitement that comes with a new task to take up, new people to engage, new challenges to face. The repetition of the daily grind wears on us, tempting us to think that nothing ever changes unless we break out of our routine and change the conditions of our everyday life. When we are frustrated by life's difficulties, afraid we're not measuring up, ambition whispers, "Maybe you're not doing what you were made for. Maybe your talent could shine brighter if you were doing something else."

Preserved among the sayings of the desert tradition is the story of a young man who came to Abba Arsenius, frustrated by his inability to do the basic tasks of monastic life. He reported: "My thoughts trouble me, saying, 'You can neither fast nor work; at least go and visit the sick, for this is also charity.'"

Listening to the young man's thoughts, Abba Arsenius recognized the voice of ambition. Visiting the sick is, of course, a good thing to do. But Arsenius knew that this young man didn't need to leave his cell to start a hospice ministry. He needed to detox from the drug of adrenaline, doing the simple things he was given to do in the place where God had called him to stay put. "Go eat, drink, sleep, do not work, only do not leave your cell," he told him. In short, just do your knitting.

The tension between fidelity and ambition is evident in the decisions we all make about our own personal development. Even if we're committed to stick with people in the place where we are, ambition tempts us to invest our best energy in something more exciting than the daily tasks of cooking meals, cleaning the church, taking care of children, doing the laundry, planning a block party, or keeping the books. At the end of a long day, an activity as banal as Web surfing can seem more exciting than conversation with a friend or neighbor. Who hasn't been distracted in the midst of a normal exchange with the person in front of them by the thought, "Maybe I should check my e-mail"?

Reflecting on the challenges to monastic stability over time, Michael Casey notes that "personal presence within the community does not exactly correspond with bodily presence." Those who have promised stability know it is possible to stay in a place without really being there. "One can continue to remain within the enclosure, but roam at will throughout the world by fantasy," Casey observes. To do so, however, is to give into the lack of care that is the principal temptation of acedia. Careful attention to the mundane tasks of daily life is the process by which we exorcise ambition and grow in love. If we really want to make a difference, stability's wisdom says to our ambition, we must learn what it means for each of us to do the knitting of life together with God's people.

Boredom's Rut

The midday demons are stubborn. They do not give up easily, but rather meet our response to their temptation by re-presenting the same lack of care under a different guise. If ambition tempts us to a hyperactivity that fragments our focus and distracts us from daily tasks, another of acedia's faces—boredom—invites us to adopt a carelessness that exhibits nearly opposite symptoms. Up to our neck in the details of daily life, we find that boredom paralyzes us, sapping the energy that seemed to flow in excess when ambition was our foe. Boredom plays Dr. Jekyll to ambition's Mr. Hyde, tempting us to despair in the murky darkness of a night that is devoid of stars. When boredom attacks, the last thing we want to hear is a challenge to do the knitting with a renewed zeal. All our zeal is gone. We'd rather crawl into a hole and let the daily grind bury us under the dust of its endless activity.

Kathleen Norris, a Benedictine oblate and spiritual writer, testifies to the way discovering monastic wisdom about acedia in midlife opened her eyes to the spiritual struggle that had plagued her since adolescence. Recalling a thought from a lunch break in early high school, she writes, "I became intensely aware of time, in a new and comfortless way. . . . Suddenly, the future seemed oppressive, even monstrous. Deeply discouraged, but unable to explain why I should feel defeated before I had even begun to live as an adult, I felt foolish and alone." Not yet knowing how to name it, Norris had already begun to hear boredom whisper its despairing cry.

But like most everyone else around her, Norris moved on with life, trying to forget her troubling thoughts and get on to the achievements that were expected of her. She kept her gaze focused on the future, self-satisfied in her natural aptitude and frustrated by things that seemed to slow her down. Despite her mother's insistence, she couldn't see the point of making her bed or doing a host of other routine activities that would only have to be repeated again the next day. Like a marionette in ambition's hands, she learned to follow its every prodding, dancing feverishly to the tune of unlimited freedom in the spiritual realm of ideas.

Inevitably, though, her body would get tired. When Norris stopped to get the rest that she could no longer deny she needed, she was confronted with an unexplainable restlessness that led to weariness and despair, making her both unable to relax and unable to do the simplest tasks. She would lie on her sofa, a book in hand, unable to read, unable to answer the phone, unable even to turn the light off and get a good night's sleep. The more "rest" she got, the more tired she felt. She was stuck in boredom's rut.

Anyone who has ever come home from a long-awaited and much-needed vacation, frustrated by a seeming inability to relax, can appreciate the honesty of Norris's confession. Caught up in a culture that rewards achievement with time off to enjoy leisure somewhere else, most of us know the feeling of being torn between ambition's frenetic activity and boredom's desperate restlessness. The practice of stability does not resolve but rather intensifies this tension, forcing us to confront the insanity that we often sustain through a bipolar vacillation between acedia's extremes. Challenged to pursue stability of heart by embracing everyday tasks here and now, we face boredom without the comfort of knowing we'll be back in the saddle next week, surrounded by new stimuli. Having committed to move forward by staying put, we must deal with the fact that we *are* in the saddle and the scenery is not changing. We've gotten ourselves into a rut.

Søren Kierkegaard articulates the depths of despair that we can descend to when life feels like one thing after another without anything to interrupt the monotony. "I do not care for anything," the Danish philosopher wrote in his description of boredom. "I do not care to ride, for the exercise is too violent. I do not care to walk, walking is too strenuous. I do not care to lie down, for I should either have to remain lying, and I do not care to do that, or I should have to get up again, and I do not care to do that either. Summa summarum: I do not care at all." Whereas ambition pushes us toward perpetual motion, boredom paralyzes, leaving us unable to love our neighbors or even take care of our own basic needs. Though different in character, these midday twins tempt us to the same lack of care. In their grip, it is impossible for us to find joy in community.

In a conversation about Jesus' instruction to welcome strangers, a Benedictine friend once confessed to me that the real challenge of hospitality is opening the door again and again to the brothers he lives with. "We Benedictines are supposed to welcome everyone as Christ," he said, "but sometimes when a brother comes through the door I mumble to myself, 'O Christ, it's *you* again.'" I laughed at the joke because I know too well how spiritual boredom can lead to a quiet disdain for the people I share life with. Little habits and phrases wear on my nerves as I ignore the needs of the people I have promised myself to in marriage, baptism, and community life. Washing their dishes makes me weary, and I avoid conversation. The thought of going on like this forever is overwhelming.

Boredom tempts us to give up on the people God has given us. But simply walking away from our commitments usually requires too much initiative when we are weighed down by the heaviness of life. Instead of taking decisive action, we give in to pettiness. I know an intentional community that lived together for a decade, sharing resources and embracing one another as family. Some years ago it dissolved, however, the individuals and families moving on to lick their wounds and pursue other things. I asked one of the former members what he thought it was that had split the group apart. "Orange juice," he said. "We couldn't agree on what kind of orange juice to buy." The disagreement was, no doubt, the culmination of a thousand irreconcilable differences. But each of them seen by itself might well seem just as petty. When spiritual boredom sets in, we fight over the smallest things, unable to care for the other person whose will is bumping up against our own.

What does stability's wisdom prescribe when we are stuck in boredom's quagmire? The angel who visited Antony in the desert demonstrated a model of alternating between the spiritual work of prayer and the manual work of weaving as an antidote for acedia. Those of us who rely on factories for our clothing and industrial farms for our food could learn something from the realism of desert spirituality: our spirits do well when our bodies have work to do. Spiritual boredom can easily be confused with depression, which should be treated as a physiological illness by doctors who can prescribe medicine that helps. But when spiritual boredom is really what we're up against, the best treatment may also be physical.

A friend who was in graduate school confessed that he was overwhelmed by sexual temptation. When he described the thoughts he had while reading in the library, it became clear that his real problem was boredom. Though he had been driven to study by the love of learning, the leisure afforded him for the purpose of scholarship was more than his young body could handle. He needed some work to do. We invited him to weed our garden for an hour every evening. He reported that the sexual temptations subsided and he actually enjoyed reading again. We noticed that our garden looked better than it ever had before.

While manual labor is no panacea for the ills of acedia, almost anything that gets our bodies moving can be a real help for spirits that grow weary in the unprecedented leisure of postindustrial society. We can be grateful that technology has reduced the burden of backbreaking work, while at the same time acknowledging the way human community depends on a healthy rhythm of working together with our spirits and our bodies. Neil, who pastors a church community known for its vibrant life together, was invited to talk to a suburban megachurch about community during their Sunday morning worship. During the question and answer time, someone asked what their commuter church could do to find more authentic community. "Have a potluck dinner once a month," Neil said.

Our lack of genuine community, rooted in acedia, may only be cured by a prescription as physical as cooking, getting tables out, eating, feeding kids, cleaning up, and asking, "Who's going to make sure this happens next month?" When we put our bodies to work to share a meal together, we may find that our spirits are renewed to sing and pray together in worship. Spiritual boredom subsides, and we have the opportunity to enjoy one another again. It may even feel natural to stand up and praise God in such a setting—an activity both spiritual and physical, if the psalms are any indication. Our spiritual health, stability's wisdom insists, depends on our hands finding good work to do. A spiritual rut can become a route to genuine growth if we remember that Jacob's ladder touches both heaven and the stuff of earth.

Vainglory's Delusion

If acedia is the lack of care that tempts us when we stay in a place, vainglory is the evil thought that suggests that we should care only about our own success. "There is ever the danger of stability giving false witness," notes Helen Lombard, a Benedictine who has served as spiritual leader of the Good Samaritan Sisters in Australia. Once we have given ourselves to stability, she observes, there is the danger of "it leading us on a path of temptation towards institutional security rather than the joy and risk of commitment to the Kingdom." Having served as a leader in her community, Lombard knows firsthand the temptations of institutional life. Stability in an established community can give occasion for the thought that our primary responsibility is institutional maintenance. Vainglory comes midway along our journey to suggest that all our care is best directed toward self-preservation.

The early monastic scholar Evagrius Ponticus wrote that vainglory is a subtle thought that "readily grows up in souls of those who practice virtue." Solitary ascetics could identify vainglory, Evagrius said, when they imagined telling the story of their struggle and becoming a hero like the saints who had first inspired them. Captivated by such a thought, they would not be tempted to flee, but rather to stay for all the wrong reasons, fueling their hyperreligious life with illusions of the glory they might achieve by staying the course and becoming a "real" ascetic. For someone so deceived, Evagrius knew that stability had become a means for idolatry.

Even if the daily disciplines of our spiritual lives are quite different from those of the desert tradition, we can learn a great deal from the dynamics of temptation that they experienced firsthand. If we embrace stability as a countercultural virtue and persevere in the practice of it for even a few years, we may hear vainglory whisper, "Don't give up; people will notice soon." And when they notice, we imagine, our having stayed will make all the difference in their lives. It will fix their marriages, heal their wounded spirits, halt global warming, or even inspire world peace. "I have observed the demon of vainglory being chased by nearly all the other demons," Evagrius wrote, "and when his pursuers fell, shamelessly he drew near and unfolded a long list of his virtues." Vainglory will try to persuade us that there is nothing more important in the world than our own stability, encouraging us to defend it at all costs against any potential threat.

But despite the incredible effort and endurance vainglory may inspire, it cannot last. "When in this way he is carried aloft by vain hope," Evagrius wrote of the monk who succumbs to thoughts of his own future greatness, "the demon vanishes and the monk is left to be tempted by the demon of pride or of sadness who brings upon him thoughts opposed to his hopes." Whether our stability gets anyone's attention or not, it cannot bear fruit if it is fueled by the false energy of vainglory. If, as we vainly hoped, people do eventually notice us, we will be consumed by a pride that insists we do not need the God we set out to love in the first place. If, on the other hand, others ignore us, we will be overcome by a sadness that makes any further effort seem impossible. This sadness is almost always the ultimate end of false stability, given that we all have to die. Without the life that knows no end in the One we call eternal, every individual and communal attempt to build a mighty fortress is in vain. "Unless the LORD builds the house," the psalmist writes, "those who build it labor in vain."

Awareness of vainglory's delusion reminds us to ask how much of the stability we invest in—good education, stable jobs, and even our ideal of family—is an attempt to establish security for ourselves apart from dependence on another's grace? If we are to practice true stability, we must find ways to receive it over and again as a gift. Rich or poor, we cannot get away from our fundamental need for a home in the household of God.

At a gathering of Benedictines from across North America, I listened with interest to a panel on contemporary expressions of monastic life. Having sat through more than a few conversations with worried denominational leaders about declining church numbers in North America, I was struck by the honesty and hope with which the monks and nuns discussed the same realities in their own communities.

"What do you like most about your community?" someone asked in the question and answer time. "We do death well," one sister said. A young woman who had recently made her vows, she went on to describe the beauty of women washing the body of one of their sisters, carrying her into the chapel, celebrating her life in their midst, and laying her to rest with the other sisters in the well-kept cemetery on the monastic grounds. Looking at the numbers, no one was sure how this community will go on when this generation has passed. That those who are there die well, however, is the most compelling witness to their newest member.

True stability is not, in the end, a way out of the mess that our world is in. If stability were but a way to build an impregnable fortress where we can be certain we are safe, it would be little more than a form of escape. But even death can be a gift if it reminds us that we must find stability beyond ourselves and our capacity to stand against the winds of change. In the desert, we are told, the early monastics made it a practice to dig a shovelful of their own grave before lying down to sleep each night. Doing so, they mocked the demons who had assaulted them at midday and they found sweet rest in the Lord.

Sitting and Rising Again

I notice in the lower right-hand corner of my computer screen that it's five past noon. The couple that was supposed to meet me for lunch hasn't shown up yet, and I'm glad.

I've been up since 5 AM, trying to write my thousand words before morning prayer, before JaiMichael woke up, before the phone started ringing or somebody came asking for a ride. I kept the lights off when it was still dark outside so as not to attract any passersby who might take seriously our door knocker that says, "I was a stranger and you welcomed me." When I got up to refill my cup of tea before anyone else was stirring, I was careful to roll my feet from heel to toe as I practiced in high school marching band, cursing the floor boards that creaked beneath my weight. When the phone rang in the late morning, I looked at the caller ID and let it go to voice mail. Was that the folks I'm supposed to have lunch with? If it was, they'll call back.

A year ago, when I was working on a book about money, a friend invited me to an all-expense-paid writing retreat by a pristine lake, a thousand miles from here. He even sent a picture. Uninterrupted time to write in a place where the only sound before lunch is the call of a loon sounded like heaven to me. I jumped at the opportunity, loved the week, and enthusiastically sent the chapter I'd written while there to my editor after I got home. Her reply: "It's missing the energy of your other chapters." My ideal is almost always an illusion, but I'm a slow learner.

The clock says ten after twelve—still no couple—and I begin to think I might just work through lunch, making notes for the class I'm teaching this afternoon. If I finish that during lunch, I might have time for . . .

I hear a car pull up outside. The couple had written to say they read a book I wrote three years ago. It touched them, they started talking to one another about changing some things in their life, and they wondered if I might have time to get together when they were in town to visit family. What more could a writer hope for? But now they're here, coming up the stairs, a little late, and I've spent the last ten minutes hoping they were lost. "Welcome," I say as I meet them at the door, hoping they can't see that I don't mean it.

I cut fresh tomatoes and put a little butter in a frying pan. "Grilled tomato and cheese OK?" They nod, slow to take the seats I've offered them at our kitchen table. The conversation is awkward, alternating between general get-to-know-you questions and the specifics of whether anyone would like ice

in their water. The table set, we bow our heads. Without thinking much about it, I ask the Holy Spirit to be with us. An hour later the wife says to me, "Didn't you say you have a class to teach at one?" It's already five minutes past, but I'm engrossed in conversation with a couple whose sincere faith has awakened me. I am born again.

The couple comes with me to class, and I enjoy teaching more than I have in months. We close with a prayer, as I usually do, but this time the hair on my arms stands up as I ask God to bless those who've gathered here today. I've no doubt that God blesses when I don't feel anything, but today my whole body is light and I want to smile because I know that I have been blessed—and all the more because I don't deserve it.

When the rest of the class is gone, I walk the couple to their car, still parked in front of our house. They thank me for my time, and I thank them too, though I cannot imagine they understand the gift they've been. Sometimes there are no words.

I climb the stairs to our front porch and turn to wave good-bye. As they drive away I pick up the yellow-handled broom that leans against the wall beside our front door. I've been sitting and talking long enough. Swinging the broom across dusty boards, I sing a work song handed down in our church, crafted to restore the spirit's hope: "Swing low, sweet chariot, coming for to carry me home. . . ."

6

BLOOMING IN THE DESERT

At a Benedictine monastery in rural Minnesota, I saw through the eyes of an abbot how a place is transformed by stability. He and I had traveled one town over to visit a friend and were returning to the monastic grounds. Driving familiar roads, he stopped once and rolled down his window to talk to a neighbor in town. As we came up the long driveway toward the abbey church, he told me about a brother who had recently died. A forestry major in college, this brother had joined the community as a young man and served it in various capacities throughout his life there. With his eye trained to see ecosystems, he noticed early on that the forests surrounding the monastery were not native to the place, but had been planted on drained wetlands by the settler monks a century before him. He suggested to the community that they might work to restore the natural habitat. They considered it for a number of years before deciding to take up the long-term project. Decades later, the abbot who was recalling this history drove us across a little bridge over a hundred-acre marsh. "The place looked completely different when I came here," he said to me.

Whatever may be said in praise of stability's more conservative virtues—its ability to preserve tradition and strengthen the things that remain—those who have practiced stability through the ages attest to its fundamental revolutionary character. Stay put and pay attention—learn to trust God in the place where you are—and you will have a front seat for the revolution that Christian tradition calls conversion. Stability transforms us along with the place where we are. Georges Chopiney, a twentieth-century Benedictine in France, summed up stability's revolutionary power:

> "What a life! What are you doing in your chrysalis!" asked brother snail, who was cheerfully dragging his shell to the four corners of the world. "I am pushing out my wings," replied the night butterfly from its chrysalis. "You will never have them because they are a gift from God to those who are stable."

Like brother snail, our mobile world mocks stability's tactic of changing the world by rooting ourselves in the ground beneath our feet and in the God who walked among us. The irony, of course, is that our technological progress drags the shell of human nature, affording us more complex and complicated means of remaining as we always have been. The twentieth century, which began with incredible optimism about the power of nonviolence and the potential for global peace manifest in Gandhi's independence movement, ended with a greater death toll than any century before it and the threat of nuclear holocaust at the touch of a single button. Though the fall of communism was celebrated by many as the "end of history"—the ultimate victory for democracy and a free market—we are terrified by the twenty-first century's defectors who would rather blow themselves up than enjoy the pursuit of happiness. Progress has not exorcised all of Cain's demons. Abel's blood still cries out from the ground beneath us.

Lest we think self-destructive violence is an anomaly among extremists, we should also note the statistics that suggest almost half of Americans are active in some form of addiction. According to recent studies, 23 million Americans are hooked on alcohol or drugs, another 61 million smoke cigarettes, and millions more are addicted to gambling, pornography, sex, and compulsive eating. Like codependent partners, the rest of us either deny the problem or find some satisfaction in being needed by people who are more obviously messed up. We are deeply broken—all of us—longing to rise up from this denial of our humanity and fly with the kingfishers and the angels. But we are all too often brother snail, unable to even imagine wings, mocking sister butterfly in her apparent confinement and dependence.

Stability cuts through our self-satisfied complacency with the radical insistence that we can, like sister butterfly, be born again. Marred though it may be, our world has not been abandoned but rather embraced by a God who saves us by refusing to leave the place where we are—by drawing closer, even, to our self-inflicted violence and suffering it on the cross. "The life, death, and resurrection of Jesus teach us that even unknown people can be touched anywhere in the world through the spiritual quality of a person who is totally faithful to God's will in his or her life, even to the point of being killed by that fidelity," writes Benedictine theologian Augustine Roberts. The incarnation—that God took on human flesh to save the whole world—is the ultimate testimony to the revolutionary power of stability. "Unless a kernel of wheat falls into the earth and dies, it remains alone," Jesus said. "But if it dies, it bears much fruit." Burying herself in the catacomb of her chrysalis, sister butterfly receives the gift of flight that brother snail cannot imagine. She is transformed by stability, made new by the grace God gives to those who stay put.

To Become a Blessing

The revolutionary power of stability resounds throughout the story of God's people, pointing us to the true end of history. When Israel is in Egypt, oppressed by a world superpower, God does not stir up a slave rebellion or send in a liberating force from elsewhere. Instead, Moses says to the people, "Do not be afraid, stand firm, and see the deliverance that the LORD will accomplish. . . . The LORD will fight for you, and you have only to keep still." The Promised Land—a place on earth for God's people to practice stability—is delivered to Israel by miraculous provision, not military might. Never meant to be a mighty fortress, Israel is defended by Gideon's unarmed soldiers and a shepherd boy with a slingshot—a constant reminder that stability depends on God alone. When God's people choose to trust in the technology of chariots and progressive political alliances rather than the Lord who delivers them, Israel is scattered. Rather than conclude that their God has been defeated, though, the prophets declare that exile is God's judgment and that stability of all things is their only hope for salvation.

Stability as the revolutionary tactic of exiles is a gift from Israel's story to those of us who practice our faith amid the fragments of tradition in a world indelibly marked by mobility. Like so many who were shipped off to Babylon, we experience a homesickness that can give rise to nostalgia, prompting us to dream of the good old days when the family farm kept us close to the land and the Internet had not yet captured our children. The practice of stability can so easily become a strategy for resisting change.

But the words of the prophet Jeremiah to God's people in exile remind us how subversive true stability is. Rather than admit defeat, daydream of lost stability, or rise up in rebellion, Jeremiah exhorts God's people to embrace a practice of revolutionary stability in the place where they are. "Build houses and live in them; plant gardens and eat what they produce. Take wives and have sons and daughters. . . . But seek the welfare of the city where I have sent you into exile, and pray to the LORD on its behalf, for in its welfare you will find your welfare."

Simply making a life where you are may not seem radical to us, but for God's people in exile, Jeremiah's instructions could not have been more unexpected. Writing from home, he says to brothers and sisters who have been violently displaced by their enemies, "Love the land you can only hate right now. Love your enemies who dragged you there. Learn to see how your well-being is bound up with theirs. Don't put all your hope in returning to a past that is forever lost. You can't go home again because your home has been destroyed. But God is faithful. Our God can meet us in the place where we are. The Maker of heaven and earth is here. If we are willing to believe it, this, too, is holy ground."

If we long for a lost stability, unsure of ourselves and our God in a world where the places we're from are changed whether we leave them or not, we are at least in good company. God's people have been here before. The word of the Lord to the prophet Jeremiah is a word for us too. Though the people of God are forever tied to the place of God's promise—a landscape marked with stones to remind us where Jacob's ladder found sure footing—Israel learned in exile that to be scattered is not necessarily to lose stability. For those with eyes to see, exile can become evangelism in the best sense of the word—good news for the whole world, even the God-forsaken places to which we've been exiled.

Geoff came to the United States from Australia to study at a seminary known for its missions program. He planned to endure a three-year degree among Yankees before setting off for some frontier, an ambassador for Christ with all the sensitivity of a well-trained anthropologist. In the course of his studies, he met and married Sherry, an American missionary-in-training. Together, they thought, they would set out for some distant land. As they studied and prayed, though, Jeremiah's words captivated them, transforming their vision of mission and calling them to put down roots in the place where they were. They found support to be commissioned as missionaries to their neighborhood in Lexington, Kentucky. Ten years later, when Geoff became a U.S. citizen, he wrote letters of thanks to all the people who'd helped him imagine what it could look like to live faithfully in America.

Geoff's genuine gratitude for people who have inhabited this land with care is a reminder that whatever stability we are able to practice depends on the stability of others— often others who knew its wisdom long before it occurred to us. With Jeremiah, Geoff has learned to see that such models of faithfulness can be found anywhere, even among our enemies. To imagine stability as mission is not to assume that we will change our neighbors and the broken places where we are if only we can muster the resolve to stick it out. Rather, it is to acknowledge that there is good news in *this* place—stability that we might not have seen at first, but without which we could not even begin. If God is faithful in exile and present in human flesh, then everything—every place—is now holy. We learn to enjoy the fruit of stability as we embrace God's mission where we are.

This is not to say that the mission of God never calls people to go elsewhere. For all of Jesus' attention to the local scene in Galilee, it is clear from the Gospel accounts that he meant for his disciples to get out with the message about God's kingdom, even to the "uttermost part of the earth." From the very beginning, those who have practiced stability in the way of Jesus have acknowledged a healthy tension between commitment to a place and the call to go elsewhere.

Writing about Abba Antony in his desert cell, Judith Sutera notes that he was "internally and emotionally bound to his home, but this fact did not bind him from traveling for worthy purposes to perform particular services and witnesses, albeit sometimes reluctantly." Antony's commitment not to easily leave his place was not a refusal to respond when he was genuinely needed. Indeed, we know about Antony today because of the incredible ministry of healing and reconciliation that he performed on visits to the city. Having done the hard work that stability required, he was able to serve his neighbors in ways no one could have anticipated before he went into his cell.

To grow in the practice of stability is to learn how to discern when we are called to stay and when God wants us to go. Theologian and Benedictine oblate Gerald Schlabach notes wisely that "we should expect authentic stability to nurture the virtues that allow Christians to become mobile in the best of ways—ready to hear the Abrahamic call, to live among the poor by both giving and receiving hospitality, and thus to nurture the newly deepened commitments by which

God's people make Christ present in new communities and cultures." Indeed, we might even go so far as to say that true Christian mission is not possible until we have established roots of love through the practice of stability. We need not look long at the history of Christian mission to see how easily it has been co-opted by greed, colonial interests, paternalism, and violence. Maybe none of us are safe to respond to God's call until we've stayed put long enough to face our demons.

But if stability's true aim is growth in the love of Christ, our practice of it will naturally move us beyond our own peace and security. Stability begins to bear its true fruit when we become a blessing to others. It is no accident that the small interracial community at Koinonia Farm that practiced stability against all odds through the fifties and sixties eventually gave birth to Habitat for Humanity, an international ministry that has, to date, built over 300,000 homes, providing safe and affordable housing to 1.5 million people in over 3,000 communities. Clarence Jordan could not have foreseen such an impact when he refused to flee from the violence and economic boycott of the Ku Klux Klan. But it may also be the case that a project like Habitat could never have been imagined without the faith that is born when we learn not to flee in the time of trouble.

Radical Self-Honesty

If true stability bears fruit, growing us up to become a blessing to the world around us, the monastic tradition also suggests that stability's fruit needs no marketing strategy. Word seems to get out well enough on its own. Indeed, the frustration of many a desert father was that after having committed to stay in his cell, he could no longer get away from the steady stream of people who came seeking counsel at his door. After word began to spread about his incredible spiritual power, Abba Antony retreated to his "inner mountain," a more remote location in the desert where casual seekers would be less likely to find him. If Antony's resistance to visitors seems slightly inhospitable, consider Benedict's word regarding the admission of new members to his community: "If someone comes and keeps knocking at the door, and if at the end of four or five days he has shown himself patient in bearing his harsh treatment and difficulty of entry, and has persisted in his request, then he should be allowed to enter."

From the desert on, hungry souls have sought out those whose stability bears the fruit of radical self-honesty. They come, as Benedictine scholar Columba Stewart observes, because "when the heart is opened to the light of truth, when there are no secrets, catches, or barriers, the demons have nowhere to lodge and hide, and they cannot begin their crafting of obsessions and illusions." Thus freed from the hang-ups of self-deception and obsessive introspection, those who have grown in the practice of stability are able to see and hear others clearly. Their insight into our lives is not magic. It is not the result of some supernatural enlightenment, given only to the spiritually elite. Rather, it is the long-term fruit of stability.

piritual direction and
disarms us. Letting our
e afraid to tell ourselves.
om from both shame and
uth of who we are back
f God that is stamped on
mire of sin.

direction, told me that
e wasn't sure where he
he wide space between
here someone ten miles
options seemed limited.
fellow twenty years his
ber of the parish all his
no training in spiritual
e of faith in that place
the man if he would
hat?" he asked. When
et once a week, the man
ll Evan what he heard,
the man said he was willing to try. "He's the best spiritual
director I've ever had," Evan told me.

Those who practice spiritual direction know that we never
outgrow our need for wise counsel from brothers and sisters
in community. We can share the fruit of self-honesty with
others only to the extent that we manifest our own thoughts
to a trusted friend, keeping our focus on Christ by inviting
others to dispel the illusions that so easily entangle those

who offer counsel. What church doesn't have in its memory the story of a pastor who, insecure in his own spirit, had an affair with a member who came to him for counsel?

Pride is a deceptive demon, attacking us at the very place where we are genuinely called to serve. Fear of falling victim to pride need not compel us to hold back our gifts or guard ourselves from failure, but rather to see again at this stage how stability is always dependent on community. Tied into the household of God, we can only share its hospitality with others to the extent that we remain connected to sisters and brothers who know us well enough to cover our weakness with their love.

Here again the prophet Jeremiah sees clearly the gifts that stability brings. Taking up what is perhaps the most common image for stability, he echoes the Psalter: "Blessed are those who trust in the LORD, whose trust is the LORD. They shall be like a tree planted by water, sending out its roots by the stream." Writing to a people who are thirsty for living water—for justice that rolls down like rushing waters in the desert of their exile—Jeremiah recalls the tree planted in the desert. "In the year of drought it is not anxious, and it does not cease to bear fruit." By the grace of stability, we can bear fruit, even in times of spiritual drought. But Jeremiah follows this celebration of stability's virtue with an immediate caution: "The heart is devious above all else; it is perverse—who can understand it?" Whatever help we may be able to offer someone else, we cannot trust our own fruit to sustain us. Our vitality depends on a root system beneath the surface, tying us to one another and connecting us to the deeper waters of God's sustaining presence.

From ancient Israel to the Egyptian desert to medieval Europe to the contemporary agrarian movement, the images of stability are strikingly constant, despite unique insights from each era and experience. Over and again for those who have practiced it, stability is a tree rooted in the earth, a monk seated in his cell with feet planted on the ground, a house built on a firm foundation, a ship anchored in the storm-tossed sea. In a tradition dominated by male writers, stability is consistently imaged as the constancy of a loving father.

But as with every tradition, there is the striking exception that stands out like the dot of yin in a sea of yang. The insight is no less true for being the minority report. Indeed, its power and beauty both are amplified by the contrast with something equally true, though perhaps overrepresented. In the great tradition of stability's wisdom, it takes a mother—Amma Syncletica—to see what is not denied but rather overlooked in all the dominant images: "If a bird abandons the eggs she has been sitting on, she prevents them from hatching, and in the same way monks or nuns will grow cold and their faith will perish if they go around from one place to another." The goal of all our stability is new life that can only come through the nurture of love in community.

We stay put and pay attention, as mothers know best, so that others can learn to fly.

The longer I struggle to practice stability, the more I am attracted to Mary, the Mother of God. Ancient Christians called Mary Theotokos—the God-bearer—because they understood that she was the first disciple to invite Jesus inside of her. Such welcome is as physical as a swollen belly and an aching back. Mary grounds our discipleship, demonstrating the integration of the spiritual and the material that we so desperately need.

Like Amma Syncletica's mother bird, Mary demonstrates a fragile stability, trusting God's interruption and making her nest in a borrowed manger. She does not have power to create the stable environment any mother would want for her child. But she receives the gifts she is given, settles down along the way, and does the hard work of delivering the life of the world. Any of us who have been incorporated into the body of Christ have Mary to thank for her faithfulness. In her, too, I find hope that we can receive the stability we need to root ourselves in a mobile culture and become a community for the life of the world.

COLLECTED WISDOM ON STABILITY

HAPPY ARE THOSE WHO DO NOT FOLLOW the advice of the wicked, or take the path that sinners tread, or sit in the seat of scoffers; but their delight is in the law of the LORD, and on his law they meditate day and night. They are like trees planted by streams of water, which yield their fruit in its season, and their leaves do not wither. In all they do, they prosper.   —Psalm 1:1–3

EVERYONE THEN WHO HEARS THESE WORDS OF MINE and acts on them will be like a wise man who built his house on rock. The rain fell, the floods came, and the winds blew and beat on that house, but it did not fall, because it had been founded on rock.   —Matthew 7:24–25

ABIDE IN ME AS I ABIDE IN YOU. Just as the branch cannot bear fruit by itself unless it abides in the vine, neither can you unless you abide in me. I am the vine, you are the branches. Those who abide in me and I in them bear much fruit, because apart from me you can do nothing.

—John 15:4–5

COME TO [JESUS CHRIST], A LIVING STONE, though rejected by mortals yet chosen and precious in God's sight, and like living stones, let yourselves be built into a spiritual house.   —1 Peter 2:4–5a

FINALLY, BE STRONG IN THE LORD and in the strength of his power. Put on the whole armor of God, so that you may be able to stand against the wiles of the devil. For our struggle is not against enemies of blood and flesh, but against the rulers, against the authorities, against the cosmic powers of this present darkness, against the spiritual forces of evil in the heavenly places. Therefore take up the whole armor of God, so that you may be able to withstand on that evil day, and having done everything, to stand firm.   —Ephesians 6:10–13

SOMEONE ASKED ABBA ANTONY, "What must one do in order to please God?" The old man replied, "Pay attention to what I tell you: whoever you may be, always have God before your eyes; whatever you do, do it according to the testimony of the holy Scriptures; in whatever place you live, do not easily leave it. Keep these three precepts and you will be saved."   —Abba Antony

SOMEONE SAID TO ABBA ARSENIUS, "My thoughts trouble me, saying, 'You can neither fast nor work; at least go and visit the sick, for this is also charity.'" But the old man, recognizing the suggestions of the demons, said to him, "Go eat, drink, sleep, do not work, only do not leave your cell." For he knew that steadfastness in the cell keeps a monk in the right way. —Abba Arsenius

SIT IN YOUR CELL and your cell will teach you everything. —Abba Moses

IF A TRIAL COMES UPON YOU in the place where you live, do not leave that place when the trial comes. Wherever you go, you will find that what you are running from is ahead of you. So stay until the trial is over, so that if you do end up leaving, no offense will be caused, and you will not bring distress to others who live in the same neighborhood. —Anonymous wisdom of the desert tradition

THERE WAS A MONK, who, because of the great number of his temptations said, "I will go away from here." As he was putting on his sandals, he saw another man who was also putting on his sandals and this other monk said to him, "Is it on my account that you are going away? Because I go before you wherever you are going." Amma Theodora

IF A BIRD ABANDONS THE EGGS SHE HAS BEEN SITTING ON, she prevents them from hatching, and in the same way monks or nuns will grow cold and their faith will perish if they go around from one place to another. —Amma Syncletica

THIS IS THE MOST MARVELOUS THING OF ALL: how the same thing is both a standing still and a moving. I mean by this that the firmer and the more immovable one remains in the Good, the more he progresses in the course of the virtues. It is like using the standing still as if it were a wing while the heart flies upward through its stability in the Good. —Gregory of Nyssa

WE SHOULD REMAIN WITHIN THE LIMITS imposed by our basic needs and strive with all our power not to exceed them. For once we are carried a little beyond these limits in our desire for the pleasures of life, there is then no criterion by which to check our onward movement, since no bounds can be set to that which exceeds the necessary.

—St. Nilus of Ancyra

WHEN WE HAVE USED [THE TOOLS OF THE SPIRITUAL CRAFT] without ceasing day and night and have returned them on judgment day, our wages will be the reward the Lord has promised: "What the eye has not seen nor the ear heard, God has prepared for those who love him" (1 Cor. 2:9). The workshop where we are to toil faithfully at these tasks is the enclosure of the monastery and stability in community.　　—Benedict of Nursia

WHEN [THE NOVICE] IS TO BE RECEIVED, he comes before the whole community in the oratory and promises stability, fidelity to monastic life, and obedience.　　—Benedict of Nursia

THOSE WHO LIVE IN HER [THE UNIVERSAL CHURCH] are not those who come and go but those who persevere in rooted stability of their spirit. —Cassidorus

THINGS WHICH HAPPEN under the condition of time are in the future, not yet in being, or in the present, already existing, or in the past, no longer in being. But God comprehends all these in a stable and eternal present. God's knowledge has no change or variation. "With him there is no alternation, or shadow of movement (James 1:17)."

　　　　　　　　　—Augustine of Hippo

JUST AS ANY YOUNG TREE, if frequently transplanted or often disturbed by being torn up after having recently been planted in a particular place, will never be able to take root, [and] will rapidly

wither and bring no fruit to perfection, similarly an unhappy monk, if he often moves from place to place at his own whim, or remaining in one place is frequently agitated by hatred of it, never achieves stability with roots of love, grows weary in the face of every useful exercise and does not grow rich in the fruitfulness of good works.

—Anselm of Canterbury

IF THEY KEEP THE FIRST VOW [stability] they are held by the content of the second [the monastic way of life]. If they keep the second, they are bound by the constraints of the first. —Peter the Venerable

IT IS NOT AT ALL SAFE to leave a certain good for an uncertain hope . . . since what we easily desire when we do not have it often becomes unbearable once experienced, for we unreasonably want a thing one minute and reject it in the next.

—Bernard of Clairvaux

THE PROUD OF HEART REJECT WISDOM when they meet her. Others, like Solomon, let themselves be drawn away from her by the delights of the flesh. Still others, losing themselves in trifles through inconstancy of their heart, abandon her, being put out by the slightest difficulty. Why do they abandon her? Because they have not sunk the roots necessary to stabilize them. Yet how can they sink roots if they do not remain in the same place? Truly, the just person planted in the house of the Lord can become rooted and built upon charity only by remaining stable in one place. This is because he will not flourish or bear lasting fruit unless he sinks deep roots. —Guerric of Igny

PEOPLE WHO WISH TO DISPEL from themselves the wicked spirits who urge them to be constantly changing and desire to flee their punishments should, if they be laypeople, collect themselves to lead a spiritual life, and if they be claustrals, let them confine themselves more strictly than usual in their way of life with all the discipline that truth requires, so that they can cast off the wickedness of this vice. —Hildegard of Bingen

WHEN WE ARE IN THE HEART, we are at home; when we are not in the heart, we are homeless.
                                    —Theophan the Recluse

LEARN TO LOVE THE PEOPLE AROUND YOU, see them with the eyes of God, and accept them as God does.   —Sr. Aquinata Böckmann

ABOVE ALL, TRUST IN THE SLOW WORK OF GOD.

We are quite naturally impatient in everything
   to reach the end without delay.

We would like to skip the intermediate stages.
We are impatient of being on the way
   to something unknown,
      something new.

And yet, it is the law of all progress
   that it is made by passing through
   some stages of instability—
      and that it may take a very long time.

Above all, trust in the slow work of God,
   our loving vine-dresser.

—Pierre Teilhard de Chardin

NO ONE HAS A CALL SIMPLY TO A PARTICULAR PLACE, as
good as it may be. The call of God is to the Will
of God. Consequently, though every institution
mediates the call of God for us, every vocation
transcends any particular institution.

—Sr. Joan Chittister

Author's note: while the stories I've told are, to the best of my knowledge, true, I've changed the names of real people in this book to protect their privacy.

CHAPTER 1

8   "When the foundations . . . " is quoted from Psalm 11:3.

10 Mobility data taken from a report by Hope Yen, "Americans not on the move," *Durham Herald Sun*, April 24, 2009.

11 Wendell Berry is quoted from his essay "In Distrust of Movements," *Resurgence* 198 (Jan/Feb 2000): 16.

12 Lao-tzu was quoted in Jean Leclercq's essay "In Praise of Stability," *Monastic Studies* 13 (Autumn 1985): 90.

14 Jacob's story is summarized from Genesis 27–28; direct quotes are from Genesis 28:13 and 28:16–17.

16 The psalmists' cries for home are taken from Psalm 5:6, Psalm 23:7, and Psalm 84:11.

17 Ephesians' image of God's people being built together into a household is quoted from 2:19–22.

18 Thomas Merton is quoted from his *The Monastic Journey* (Kansas City: Sheed, Andrews, & McMeel, 1977), 68.

21 Michael Casey is quoted from "The Value of Stability," *Cistercian Studies Quarterly* 31 (1996): 291.

24 The first quotation from Clarence Jordan is taken from Charles Marsh, *The Beloved Community* (New York: Basic Books, 2005), 78. The second, from a letter to his son, is quoted in my *Inhabiting the Church* (Eugene, OR: Cascade Books, 2007), 36.

25 The Dorothy Bass quotation is from a conversation with the author, and is used with her permission.

31 "My heart is firmly fixed . . . " is a quote from Psalm 57:7.

32 Amma Syncletica's gem can be found in Benedicta Ward, trans., *The Sayings of the Desert Fathers* (Kalamazoo, MI: Cistercian Publications, 1984), 231.

CHAPTER 2

33 "The Lord is in his holy temple . . . " is quoted from Habakuk 2:20.

35 Abba Antony's quote is taken from Ward, *Sayings of the Desert Fathers*, 2.

35 The second quote from the desert tradition is Anonymous 68, translated by Rowan Williams in *Where God Happens: Discovering Christ in One Another* (Boston: New Seeds, 2005), 99.

37 Luke's Gospel tells the story of Jesus' meeting the Gerasene demoniac in 8:26–39.

37 "Sitting at the feet . . . " is quoted from Luke 8:35.

38 "Return to your home . . . " is quoted from Luke 8:39.

39 "Not against flesh . . . " is taken from Ephesians 6:12.

42 The quotation from the *Rule of Saint Benedict* (RB) 7:5–6 is taken from the 1980 edition, edited by Timothy Fry (Collegeville, MN: Liturgical Press, 1981).

43 ". . . this descent and ascent . . . " is quoted from RB 7:7.

43 "Stability, fidelity to monastic life . . . " is taken from RB 58:17.

43 Barbara Kingsolver's reflection on asparagus and stability is taken from her *Animal, Vegetable, Miracle* (New York: Harper Perennial, 2008), 28.

45 Wendell Berry is quoted from his *Jayber Crow* (New York: Counterpoint, 2000), 281.

48 G.R. Evans, trans., *Bernard of Clairvaux: Selected Works*, The Classics of Western Spirituality (New York: Paulist Press, 1987), 120.

49 "It was better for Jacob . . . " is from the same, 121.

49 William of Saint Thierry's treatise *On the Nature and Dignity of Love* is quoted in M. Basil Pennington, *A School of Love* (Harrisburg, PA: Morehouse Publishing, 2000), 18.

51 Charles Cummings is quoted from his *Monastic Practices* (Kalamazoo, MI: Cistercian Publications, 1986), 175.

57 "As shoes for your feet . . . " is taken from Ephesians 6:15.

CHAPTER 3

59 "The workshop where we are to toil faithfully . . . " is a quote from RB 4:78.

60 Peter the Venerable is quoted from Giles Constable, ed., *The Letters of Peter the Venerable* (Cambridge, MA: Harvard University Press, 1967), I, 55.

61 "Come unto me . . . " is from Matthew 11:30.

62 Rowan Williams is quoted from his book *Where God Happens*, 11.

65 "Energetic as they were . . . " is taken from RB 18:25.

66 "Happy are those . . . " is quoted from Psalm 1:1–3.

67 "O LORD, how many are my foes!" is from Psalm 3:1.

67   "It is not enemies who taunt me . . . " is quoted from Psalm 55:12–14.

67   "Will you forget me forever?" and "I will sing to the LORD . . . " are taken from Psalm 13, verses 1 and 6 respectively.

68   "I will sing praises . . . " is from Psalm 146:2.

68   Lazare de Seilhac's reflections are quoted from "The Dynamism of a Living Stability," *Benedictines* 47 (1994): 46.

71   Maggie Jackson is quoted from her book *Distracted* (Amherst, NY: Prometheus Books, 2008), 84. Gloria Mark's research on "interruption science" is also taken from Jackson's book.

71   Augustine is quoted from *City of God* 11:21 (New York: Penguin Books, 1984), 452.

73   The story of Sant'Egidio is told by Thomas Cahill in his *A Saint on Death Row* (New York: Doubleday, 2009), 38.

CHAPTER 4

82   Anselm of Canterbury is quoted from Walter Froelich, trans., *The Letters of St. Anselm of Canterbury*, vol. 1, CS 96 (Kalamazoo, MI: Cistercian Publications, 1990), 134.

85   "The boundary lines . . . " is taken from Psalm 16:6.

86   Paul Wilkes is quoted from his article "Stability: A Sense of Where You Are," *Benedictines* 51:1 (Spring/Summer 2001): 23, 31.

87   Michael Casey is quoted from his book *Strangers to the City* (Brewster, MA: Paraclete Press, 1996), 189.

90, 92   Augustine Roberts is quoted from his book *Centered on Christ* (Kalamazoo, MI: Cistercian Publications, 2005), 240–41.

93 Amma Theodora's story is quoted from Ward, *Sayings of the Desert Fathers*, 84.

95 Jean Vanier's story and quote are taken from Jean Vanier and Stanley Hauerwas, *Living Gently in a Violent World* (Downers Grove, IL: InterVarsity Press, 2008), 31.

97 "Abide in me . . . " is quoted from John 15:4.

97 Jesus' teachings of forgiveness are quoted from Matthew 18.

106 Lee Edwin Kiser's "Rough Weather Makes Good Timber" is quoted with permission from Patsy M. Ginns, *Rough Weather Makes Good Timber: Carolinians Recall* (Chapel Hill, NC: University of North Carolina Press, 1977).

CHAPTER 5

107 "Be strong in the Lord . . . " is quoted from Ephesians 6:10.

108 John Cassian's quotes from *The Institutes* are taken from Kathleen Norris, *Acedia and Me* (New York: Riverhead, 2008), 289.

109 Antony's struggle with acedia is recorded in Ward, *Sayings of the Desert Fathers*, 1–2.

110 "With fear and trembling" refers to Philippians 2:12.

111 The story about Gordon Cosby and Church of the Savior is recounted from conversations with church members and Michelle Boorstein, "Activist D.C. Church Embraces Transition in Name of Its Mission," *Washington Post*, January 6, 2009, A1.

113 The quotation from Jim Wallis is from the same *Washington Post* article mentioned in the previous note.

114 Abba Arsenius is quoted from Ward, *Sayings of the Desert Fathers*, 10.

115 Michael Casey is quoted from his article "The Value of Stability," *Cistercian Studies Quarterly* 31 (1996): 290.

116 Kathleen Norris's experience is recounted from her *Acedia and Me*, 8.

118 The quote from Søren Kierkegaard is taken from Norris, *Acedia and Me*, 16.

122 Helen Lombard's caution is quoted from her article "Stability's Amazing Paradoxes," *Benedictines* 47 (1994): 51.

122 Evagrius' thoughts on vainglory are taken from his *Praktikos* 13 and 31 (Kalamazoo, MI: Cistercian Publications, 1980), 19, 47.

124 "Unless the LORD builds . . . " is quoted from Psalm 127:1.

CHAPTER 6

134 Imagined conversation between snail and butterfly is taken from Georges Chopiney, OSB, monk of Clervaux, as quoted in Jean Leclercq, "In Praise of Stability," 98.

135 Data on addiction in America is taken from Benoit Denizet-Lewis, *Ameria Anonymous* (New York: Simon and Schuster, 2009), 12.

136 Augustine Roberts is quoted from his book *Centered on Christ*, 232.

136 "Unless a kernel . . . " is quoted from John 12:24.

136 "Do not be afraid . . . " is quoted from Exodus 14:13–14.

137 "Build houses and . . . " is quoted from Jeremiah 29:5–7.

140 "Uttermost part of the earth" is quoted from Acts 1:8, KJV.

140 Judith Sutera is quoted from her article "Place and Stability in the Life of Antony," *Cistercian Studies* (1992): 108.

140 Gerald Schlabach is quoted from his "Stability and Mobility: The Oblate's Challenge and Witness," *The American Benedictine Review* 52:1 (March 2001): 21.

141 Data about Habitat for Humanity is cited from the organization's website, www.habitat.org.

142 Benedict's instruction on admitting new members is quoted from RB 58:3–4.

142 Columba Stewart is quoted from his article "The Desert Fathers on Radical Self-Honesty," *Vox Benedicta* 8 (1991): 10.

144 "Blessed are those . . . " is quoted from Jeremiah 17:7–8a, followed by a quote from 17:8b.

144 "The heart is devious . . . " is quoted from Jeremiah 17:9.

145 Amma Syncletica quoted from Ward, *Sayings of the Desert Fathers*, 231.

COLLECTED WISDOM ON STABILITY

148 Abba Antony is quoted from Ward, *Sayings of the Desert Fathers*, 2.

149 Abba Arsenius and Abba Moses are quoted from the same, pages 10 and 139, respectively.

149 The anonymous saying is from Anonymous 68, translated by Rowan Williams in *Where God Happens*, 99.

149 Amma Theodora is quoted from Ward, *Sayings of the Desert Fathers*, 84.

150 Amma Syncletica is quoted from Ward, *Sayings of the Desert Fathers*, 231.

150 Gregory of Nyssa is quoted from Aquinata Böckmann, *Perspectives on the Rule of St. Benedict: Expanding Our Hearts in Christ* (Collegeville, MN: Liturgical Press, 2005), 135.

150 St. Nilus of Ancyra is quoted from *Ascetic Discourses*, vol. 1, *Philokalia*, 290.

150 Benedict is quoted from RB 4:76–78, p. 187, and RB 58:17, p. 269.

151 Cassidorus is quoted from Commentary on Psalm 23, quoted in Jean Leclercq, "In Praise of Stability."

151 Augustine of Hippo is quoted from *City of God*, 452.

151 Anselm of Canterbury is quoted from Froelich, *Letters of St. Anselm of Canterbury*, 134.

152 Peter the Venerable is quoted from Constable, *Letters of Peter the Venerable*, I, 55.

152 Bernard of Clairvaux quote from *On Precept and Dispensation*, chapter 16, no. 46, is taken from Augustine Roberts, *Centered on Christ*, 212.

152 Guerric of Igny is quoted from *First Sermon for the Feast of St. Benedict*, 2, quoted in Roberts, *Centered on Christ*, 220.

153 Hildegard of Bingen is quoted from *The Book of the Rewards of Life*, trans. Bruce Hozeski (New York: Oxford University Press, 1997), 42.

153 Theophan the Recluse is quoted from Timothy Ware, ed., *The Art of Prayer: An Orthodox Anthology* (London: Faber & Faber, 1971), 192.

153 Aquinata Böckmann is quoted from her *Perspectives on the Rule of St. Benedict*, 135.

154 The Pierre Teilhard de Chardin quotation is adapted from http://www.worship.ca/docs/p_62_ptdc.html, accessed on February 18, 2010.

154 Joan Chittister is quoted from her *The Rule of St. Benedict: Insights for the Ages* (New York: Crossroad, 1996), 113.

ABOUT PARACLETE PRESS

Who We Are

Paraclete Press is a publisher of books, recordings, and DVDs on Christian spirituality. Our publishing represents a full expression of Christian belief and practice—from Catholic to Evangelical, from Protestant to Orthodox.

We are the publishing arm of the Community of Jesus, an ecumenical monastic community in the Benedictine tradition. As such, we are uniquely positioned in the marketplace without connection to a large corporation and with informal relationships to many branches and denominations of faith.

What We Are Doing
Books

Paraclete publishes books that show the richness and depth of what it means to be Christian. Although Benedictine spirituality is at the heart of all that we do, we publish books that reflect the Christian experience across many cultures, time periods, and houses of worship. We publish books that nourish the vibrant life of the church and its people—books about spiritual practice, formation, history, ideas, and customs.

We have several different series, including the best-selling Living Library, Paraclete Essentials, and Paraclete Giants series of classic texts in contemporary English; A Voice from the Monastery—men and women monastics writing about living a spiritual life today; award-winning literary faith fiction and poetry; and the Active Prayer Series that brings creativity and liveliness to any life of prayer.

Recordings

From Gregorian chant to contemporary American choral works, our music recordings celebrate sacred choral music through the centuries. Paraclete distributes the recordings of the internationally acclaimed choir Gloriæ Dei Cantores, praised for their "rapt and fathomless spiritual intensity" by *American Record Guide*, and the Gloriæ Dei Cantores Schola, which specializes in the study and performance of Gregorian chant. Paraclete is also the exclusive North American distributor of the recordings of the Monastic Choir of St. Peter's Abbey in Solesmes, France, long considered to be a leading authority on Gregorian chant.

DVDs

Our DVDs offer spiritual help, healing, and biblical guidance for life issues: grief and loss, marriage, forgiveness, anger management, facing death, and spiritual formation.

Learn more about us at our website:
www.paracletepress.com,
or call us toll-free at 1-800-451-5006.

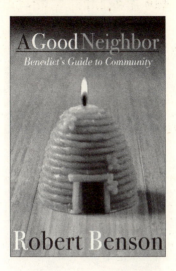

oblate
acedia

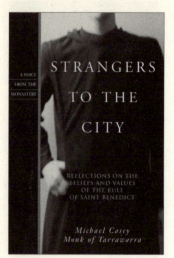